SECOND EDITION

The
Literacy
Coach's
Survival Guide

Essential Questions and
Practical Answers

Cathy A. Toll

INTERNATIONAL
Reading Association
800 BARKSDALE ROAD, PO BOX 8139
NEWARK, DE 19714-8139, USA
www.reading.org

The International Reading Association attempts, through its publications, to provide a forum for a wide spectrum of opinions on reading. This policy permits divergent viewpoints without implying the endorsement of the Association.

Executive Editor, Publications   Shannon Fortner

Acquisitions Manager   Tori Mello Bachman

Managing Editors   Susanne Viscarra and Christina M. Lambert

Editorial Associate   Wendy Logan

Creative Services/Production Manager   Anette Schuetz

Design and Composition Associate   Lisa Kochel

Art   Cover design: Lise Holliker Dykes; Cover and section opener photos: Golden Pixels, Monkey Business Images, Pressmaster, MR Gao, auremar, racorn, and Zurijeta (all Shutterstock)

Library of Congress Cataloging-in-Publication Data

Toll, Cathy A., 1956–

The literacy coach's survival guide : essential questions and practical answers / Cathy A. Toll. — Second edition.

p.   cm.

Includes bibliographical references and index.

ISBN 978-0-87207-156-8 (alk. paper)

1. Mentoring in education—United States. 2. Reading teachers—In-service training—United States. I. Title.

LB1731.4.T65   2014

371.102—dc23

2013046576

Suggested APA Reference

Toll, C.A. (2014). *The literacy coach's survival guide: Essential questions and practical answers* (2nd ed.). Newark, DE: International Reading Association.

CONTENTS

SECTION 1

Why Coaching?

SECTION 2

What Does a Successful Literacy Coach Do?

SECTION 3

How Do I Address Specific Coaching Challenges?

ABOUT THE AUTHOR

 **Cathy Toll** supports teacher learning by guiding educational coaches, professional learning teams, and administrative leaders. She has been a consultant, keynote speaker, and workshop leader throughout the United States, Australia, and Canada. Cathy has served as a teacher at the elementary, middle, and high school levels; a reading specialist; a curriculum coordinator; a school principal; a director of literacy research and development; a university faculty member; a grant director; a state department of education consultant; and an educational coach.

Cathy has published widely for teacher leaders, including four books for literacy coaches and a recent book on Learnership for principals and teacher leaders. She received her doctoral degree from Pennsylvania State University and has done research on teacher professional growth, school change, and enactments of power in educational settings.

Cathy lives in Madison, Wisconsin, with her partner, David, and two cats. Her website is www.partneringtolearn.com.

What Is This Book About?
Who Is It For?

- Why did I write this book?
- Who is the target audience for this book?
- How has coaching changed over the last decade?
- What essentials are the same as they were when I wrote the first edition of this book?
- What is in this book?
- How is the second edition different from the first?

A decade ago, I found that I had a book in me. After years of coaching teachers and coaches, I recognized that I understood some things and used some practices that were not to be found in the professional literature at the time. I began paying extra attention to my coaching practices and reflected on the underlying research, theories, and beliefs that shaped them. Soon I was drafting the first edition of this book, and I held my first copy in my hands in 2005.

I'm delighted that the first edition has been labeled a best seller by the International Reading Association, that it has been called the coaching bible by some, and that one colleague rereads it every August before starting another year as a literacy coach. The book is in large part the springboard for consulting work that I have done across the United States and in parts of Australia and Canada. It has served coaches well, and it has been deeply meaningful to me.

Over the same period of time, education has changed. No Child Left Behind has faded in impact, and Race to the Top, the Common Core State Standards, PARCC and Smarter Balanced assessments, and Response to Intervention have become focal points instead. Programs of literacy coaching have changed as well. In schools where Reading First provided the additional impetus for coaching, there is an expanded vision of what literacy coaches can do and who they can work with; in districts that began coaching at the elementary level, there is now coaching in middle and high schools as well;

and universities, regional offices of education, and state departments of education now offer training and resources for the demands of this work.

I have changed, too. Although the fundamentals of coaching remain the same for me—develop trust, communicate well, start with the teacher, develop partnerships, focus on learning—I now give greater priority to the coaching conversation and de-emphasize directing teachers toward goals or outcomes that are not their own. I hold even stronger the conviction that coaching must be separate from supervising and recognize even more that classroom observations are not essential for effective coaching. And because I now have interacted with thousands of coaches from across the world, I have an even greater appreciation for the work of coaching and an even greater sensitivity to its challenges.

It is time for the second edition.

As I wrote in the Introduction to the first edition, I want this book to provide for literacy coaches and those who work with them a great deal of practical information. In addition, I want to give literacy coaches just enough background and perspective to coach in the most effective way. Finally, I want this book to be friendly, like a conversation. I believe the best coaching takes place in a supportive relationship. Therefore, I want my voice to come through in this book so you sense me as a person who is working alongside you, helping you become the literacy coach you want to be. I still value these qualities as I write this second edition and hope you find them in this book as you read on.

Let's Get to Know Each Other

I come to this work as someone who has been a literacy educator for over 35 years. I have been a classroom teacher at the elementary, middle, high school, and postsecondary levels; a reading specialist; a district reading coordinator; an elementary school principal; a university faculty member; and a consultant to teachers, literacy coaches, administrators, and others. I have provided leadership in federal education laboratories and state departments of education.

I currently lead Partnering to Learn, an organization that specializes in serving literacy coaches and those who support them. In this capacity, I provide training workshops, one-to-one and small-group coaching, consultation, print resources, grant writing, research, and evaluation for literacy coaches and leaders of programs that include literacy coaching.

I've done a great deal of reading and some research on change in literacy education and on coaching in general. I'll confess, though, that most of what I believe about literacy coaching is influenced by my experiences. To be candid, I've made practically every possible mistake, both as a teacher and as a leader.

However, here's the good news: I work very hard to learn from my mistakes. My practical struggles have caused me to study change and the leadership of change and to develop new, more effective practices and perspectives. To my pleasant surprise, I've discovered that the insights and practices that I have developed, based on my formal education and my education in the real world of schools, enable me to coach literacy coaches with a high degree of success.

When I wrote the first edition of this book, I predicted that readers would be literacy coaches who were fairly new to their position and who likely worked in an elementary school. I do not expect that readers of this edition will necessarily fit that profile. Over the years, I have encountered math coaches, technology coaches, instructional coaches, and myriad others reading this book because so much about literacy coaching applies to other areas of coaching in education. I also assume that readers will work across the spectrum of educational levels, from those whose coaching partners are preschool teachers to those who work with university graduate students, and everything in between. At this point, interest in coaching occurs throughout our profession. As for the newness of coaches who read this book, I expect that there is a range of coaching experience. Some readers likely are new indeed, but others surely have several years' experience in coaching.

The increased diversity of coaches' work and experience is heartening because it demonstrates the widening impact that coaching has in education. I welcome coaches of all kinds to the readership of this book! I also welcome those who support coaches as program leaders, administrators, trainers, or university faculty members.

Some of you, too, will be readers of the first edition of the book who are looking for more. This second edition contains over 65% new material, so I hope you find that it enhances your work and perspectives.

I am eager to begin or continue the conversation about coaching with all of you!

The Organization of This Book

To make this book accessible, I've divided it into sections consisting of a few chapters each. I've also provided a list of questions at the beginning of each chapter to indicate which of your questions that chapter will answer.

The main part of the book is divided into three sections. Each section addresses a major group of questions asked about literacy coaching. The questions corresponding to the first section of this book address the basics of coaching: What is coaching, why does it matter, and how does it influence teachers' learning? Chapter 1 is devoted to those first two questions as well as a comparison of literacy coaches with reading specialists and mentors and a brief discussion of the need for literacy coaches.

Because coaching exists to support change, Chapter 2 considers the kinds of changes that literacy coaching might aim for and offers new perspectives on educational change itself. Chapter 3 continues in this vein by delineating how coaches might use their time for greatest influence and how they can most effectively position themselves in relation to teachers they are trying to influence.

The second section of the book focuses on practical strategies to bring about literacy coaching's potential. Chapter 4 helps coaches get off to a good start with teachers, principals, students, and parents and provides suggestions for beginning to collaborate with individuals and teams. Chapter 5 addresses communication, providing general approaches to effective communication as well as specific strategies for communicating well. Chapter 6 provides specifics on the coaching conversation, including the problem-solving cycle, coaches' tasks, and tools for record keeping. Chapter 7 is all about coaching with teams, including coaches' possible roles, adjustments in the coaching conversation, and understanding team development over time.

Specific coaching challenges are the focus of the third section. Chapter 8 helps coaches deal with difficult situations, such as resistance in teachers, intimidation in groups, problems in goal development, and coaches' own anxieties and defensiveness. Chapter 9 is about coaching for initiatives such as the Common Core State Standards and Response to Intervention; it delineates coaches' stances and strategies for helping teachers bring these initiatives to life as well as tactics to use when there is disagreement with these endeavors. Chapter 10 will help coaches who are struggling to enjoy their work and feel successful.

I end the book with an overview of activities to do and to avoid as a literacy coach in the Conclusion and with a narrative bibliography in the Appendix that provides references to which you can refer for more information on many topics that I address throughout the book.

I'd like to add a bit more about resources and references. As an author, I strive always to give credit to others whose ideas I use in my work. I do that in this book, using typical reference citations, when I specifically refer to others' work. On the other hand, much of what I write about in this book is not taken directly from the work of others but, rather, reflects my own work in the field and in theorizing and researching literacy coaching. My thinking is influenced by a wide range of reading that I have done. I would like to make you aware of that reading, both to acknowledge the contribution of other authors and to help you understand how my ideas have evolved. My concern is that if I fill the main part of the book with references to a lot of additional sources, the book may become less user-friendly. I've resolved this dilemma in two ways: First, I've included a few key resources at the end of each chapter, which will provide you with additional ideas or background information. Second, I've provided information about additional sources in the narrative bibliography.

I've attempted in this narrative bibliography to continue to talk to you, the reader, rather than just list resources. I hope that style is helpful and engaging. Of course, I also provide a traditional list of references at the end of the book.

Conclusion

There is no doubt in my mind that literacy coaching is an effective model and that the need for literacy coaches is great. A book such as this will assist literacy coaches in doing the job that lies before them.

ADDITIONAL RESOURCES

Flaherty, J. (1999). *Coaching: Evoking excellence in others.* Boston, MA: Butterworth-Heinemann.

Knight, J. (2008). *Coaching: Approaches and perspectives.* Thousand Oaks, CA: Corwin.

Rodgers, E.M., & Pinnell, G.S. (Eds.). (2002). *Learning from teaching in literacy education: New perspectives on professional development.* Portsmouth, NH: Heinemann.

Sweeney, D.R., & Harris, L.S. (2002). Learning to work with—not against—a system. *Journal of Staff Development, 23*(3), 16–19.

Toll, C.A. (2008). *Surviving but not yet thriving: Essential questions and practical answers for experienced literacy coaches.* Newark, DE: International Reading Association.

SECTION 1

Why Coaching?

CHAPTER 1

What Is Literacy Coaching?

- What exactly *is* a literacy coach?
- How are literacy coaches different from reading specialists and mentors?
- What is the value of literacy coaching?
- What is the demand for literacy coaches?

Coaching has become popular in schools these days. However, despite the proliferation of coaches and coaching programs, there is still confusion about what coaching actually is. I find that definitions of coaching range from "helping teachers do better," to "improving instruction," to "ensuring that teachers are all on the same page," to "collaborating with teacher teams to analyze data," to...well, you get the point: People understand coaching differently!

Literacy coaches often have to clarify—for themselves and others—the nature of their work. To help, I offered this definition in the first edition of this book:

> A literacy coach is one who helps teachers to recognize what they know and can do, assists teachers as they strengthen their ability to make more effective use of what they know and do, and supports teachers as they learn more and do more. (Toll, 2005, p. 4)

I'd like to point out several significant aspects of this definition. First, note that the emphasis is on teachers. Coaches' clients are teachers. Greater student achievement is the desired outcome, but coaches' focus is teachers. Note, too, that this definition is written from a positive perspective; it doesn't say that literacy coaches fix problem situations or teachers. Another feature of the definition is that it places literacy coaches in the role of supporting teachers; in other words, teachers are responsible for identifying their strengths and growing their capabilities, and literacy coaches are there to assist. Some literacy coaches and teachers believe that the literacy coach is there to tell the teachers what they should be doing and to make sure they do it. That is not at all the vision of literacy coaching that you'll find in this book.

I like this definition for all the reasons above. However, it is a bit abstract. Therefore, over the years, I developed a second definition of literacy coaching:

A literacy coach partners with teachers for job-embedded professional learning that enhances teachers' reflection on students, the curriculum, and pedagogy for the purpose of more effective decision making.

This definition provides additional important details:

- Coaching is a partnership. Coaching is a collaboration between equals. I avoid language that implies that coaching is *done to* teachers, such as when one says that a teacher *is coached* or that coaches *provide coaching* to teachers. Rather, I talk about the coaching partnership. The metaphor I find helpful is a ballroom dance, where both partners move in synchronicity, with the lead partner providing the subtlest of pressure on the back or arm of his partner. (Yes, ballroom dancing still hews to traditional gender roles!) Similarly, coaches provide the subtlest of leadership by steering the process, but truly the partners are in sync when coaching is successful.

- Coaching is job-embedded. Teachers, myself included, want to learn what matters to their work with their students in their classrooms. Coaching provides support for that kind of work.

- Coaching is about professional learning. When coaching is effective, teachers learn. I no longer talk about "professional development" when I speak of coaching because *development* sounds like something done *to* teachers. In addition, when learning is emphasized, partners in the coaching relationship are reminded what it is all about.

- Coaching supports reflection about students, the curriculum, and pedagogy. Too often, coaching processes emphasize only one aspect of the work of teaching, for instance, when coaches and teachers address only best practices or only student data. This definition is a reminder that at one time or another, coaching partnerships consider all three aspects of teachers' work: students, content, and processes.

- Coaching leads to better decisions. Literacy coaches are successful when their teacher partners make decisions that increase student learning. True, coaching might lead to higher test scores, more orderly classrooms, or calmer teachers, if those are appropriate goals in particular situations, but the outcome of all coaching should be that students are learning more of what we want them to learn because teachers are making better decisions.

Who Is a Literacy Coach?

Not everyone can be a literacy coach. Literacy coaches need to be well versed in the research, theory, and practices of literacy instruction. In addition, literacy coaches need a sound understanding of teaching, learning, and child development. Literacy coaches also need knowledge of adult learning, particularly teacher professional learning. Finally, literacy coaches need strong interpersonal skills, especially in the areas of communication and empathy, and good skills in planning and organizing. On top of all of these qualities, literacy coaches must be trustworthy so teachers are comfortable collaborating with them even when the teachers are struggling or have failed.

There is some overlap between the duties of a reading specialist and a literacy coach, and therefore these roles are sometimes confused. Both reading specialists and literacy coaches serve as building leaders in literacy instruction, and both support the goal of improving student achievement. However, reading specialists more often work with students directly and provide more support to curriculum development and implementation, whereas literacy coaches focus much more of their attention on improving student achievement by working directly with teachers. Granted, reading specialists sometimes work directly with teachers and literacy coaches sometimes work directly with students, but the latter usually happens only when demonstrating for coaches' teacher partners. In addition, members of both groups perform additional duties, such as contributing to building-level professional development workshops and advising the principal on literacy-related matters. Given these overlapping duties, it is easy to see why confusion between reading specialists and literacy coaches may occur. To make the distinctions easier, Table 1 outlines these differences.

Many individuals perform the tasks of both reading specialists and literacy coaches, either because they have a divided job, such as 50% reading specialist and 50% coach, or because they have the title of reading specialist but are asked to include coaching duties in their work. My advice to those of you with overlapping roles such as these is to monitor your time carefully to be sure that you give adequate attention to your coaching duties. Without care, many reading specialists never get around to coaching duties, or many coaches with reading specialist responsibilities as well find that their work with students consumes the time available to work with teachers.

There is also confusion at times between coaches and mentors. As with reading specialists, there is overlap between the duties of coaches and the duties of mentors. A key distinction, though, is the difference in clients. Coaches' clients are teachers: Coaching is job-embedded and focuses on teachers' challenges and interests. In contrast, mentors have several clients. Mentors work with new teachers to help them adjust to the teaching profession, learn about district and school policies and practices, and develop their teaching practice so their students learn well. Therefore, mentors' clients include administrators, teachers, and even the profession, given that mentoring has been promoted as a way to retain new teachers in the profession. Mentors sometimes attend to the challenges and interests of the new teachers they work

Table 1. Comparison of Reading Specialists and Literacy Coaches

Reading Specialists	Literacy Coaches
Support students, parents, and administrators, as well as teachers	Emphasize support for teachers, although support for others also may take place
Frequently provide direct instruction to students on a daily basis	Provide direct instruction to students primarily when demonstrating for teachers
Provide evaluations of students for a variety of reasons, including curriculum monitoring, student diagnosis, and monitoring teacher and school effectiveness	Provide evaluation of students primarily to demonstrate for teachers or to support teachers in their instructional decision making
Work directly with teachers to an extent but do not necessarily focus work on this area	Spend a great amount of time working directly with teachers in individual and small-group meetings
When working with teachers, may be responding to teachers' needs and concerns but also may be directing teachers to meet requirements or implement mandatory programs	Work with teachers mostly in response to teachers' needs and concerns

with, but mentors also attend to the curriculum, human resource information, or administrative tasks. Thus, coaching is likely one of the tactics in mentors' tool kits, but understandably, mentors must perform many other tasks as well.

Why Literacy Coaching?

With the range of experience and education that I have benefited from as an educator, I am at a point in my career that allows me to choose the focus of my work. I choose coaching, along with professional learning teams and administrative leadership of professional learning, because it has great potential. When done well, coaching helps both teachers and students be more successful.

Literacy coaching is particularly effective in supporting teachers' learning that enhances student learning because of these characteristics:

- Literacy coaching honors adult learners. Adult learners like to have a say in their learning and to have the learning process respond directly to their needs. In addition, many adults are aware of how they learn best, and most adults want their learning to be directly applicable to their lives (Cave, LaMaster, & White, 2006). The literacy coaching process honors the way adults learn by responding to teachers' needs and supporting them as they learn about topics and issues that they have selected. In addition, literacy coaching supports teachers' growth in a variety of ways, according to teachers' styles of learning, and literacy coaching allows teachers to apply and test what they are learning in the day-to-day work that they do in their classrooms.

- Literacy coaching supports collaboration. Increasingly, evidence suggests that learners rarely learn in isolation (Davis, Sumara, & Luce-Kapler, 2007). Of course, teachers have long collaborated with one another, despite the myth that teachers always close their classroom doors and work in isolation. However, time for collaborations and processes for productive collaboration have often been missing from teachers' work. Coaching provides the conditions for collaboration, and a savvy coach provides the process expertise to optimize collaborative endeavors.

- Literacy coaching promotes reflection and decision making. Many educators believe that teaching is best when teachers are reflective (Schön, 1987; Zeichner & Liston, 1996). This makes sense, doesn't it? To do a job with the complexity of teaching, it is essential to think about it carefully and deeply—not just about what is happening at the time but about why it happened, how it affects and is affected by other factors and events, and what it will affect in the future. For instance, if you try a new teaching strategy—for example, doing shared reading with students—you'll do your best teaching if you think about how your use of the strategy went, including what went well, what needs improvement, what the students did well during the activity, what they tried that they hadn't tried before, and what knowledge and strategies they used during the activity. You also should look ahead and think about whether you'd use the practice again, what you'd do the same, what you'd do differently, and so forth. All of this reflection would help you make shared reading as effective as possible.

- Literacy coaching leads to greater student achievement. The largest studies showing that literacy coaching increases student learning are a study on coaching in the Literacy Collaborative program by Biancarosa, Bryk, and Dexter (2010) and a multiyear study of literacy coaches in middle schools throughout Florida (Marsh et al., 2008). There are many smaller studies that also suggest coaching's positive effects.

Literacy coaching serves many purposes. It supports teacher professional development in a manner that honors how adults learn best. It supports teachers' collaboration, reflection, and decision making. Above all, effective literacy coaching contributes to increased student achievement. Given all the reasons for literacy coaching, the need for literacy coaches is increasing rapidly.

The Need for Literacy Coaches

Although reading specialists and others have engaged in coachlike duties for many years, it was the Reading First program, enacted as part of the No Child Left Behind Act of 2001, that placed literacy coaching in the national spotlight. A requirement of Reading First was that every school receiving funding for the program had to have a reading coach. Thus, as Reading First was implemented in thousands of elementary schools in all 50 U.S. states plus the District of Columbia, American Samoa, and schools run by the Bureau of Indian Affairs, reading coaches were hired accordingly.

Many administrators in non–Reading First schools took note of the reading coaches in their colleagues' schools and found ways to fund their own coaches. In addition, the U.S. Department of Health and Human Services advocated mentor teachers in all Head Start programs; in many of these programs, these mentors act as coaches and often are even called coaches or mentor-coaches.

Over the last decade, initiatives sponsored by education-related organizations, such as the Carnegie Corporation of New York and the Alliance for Excellent Education, have included literacy coaching, and various pieces of federal legislation, such as Striving Readers, the LEARN (Literacy Education for All, Results for the Nation) Act, and proposed reauthorizations of the Elementary and Secondary Education Act, have included literacy coaches.

Two major initiatives in the United States are also increasing the demand for literacy coaches: Response to Intervention and the Common Core State Standards. Schools and districts are turning to coaches to support teachers in implementing these initiatives to their fullest. Additionally, coaches are seen as key partners in enhancing teachers' success with students identified as English learners.

Thus, the need for literacy coaching is evident across the United States, at all levels of schooling and in many educational settings. Coaching is seen as an important method for improving literacy instruction and literacy achievement.

Conclusion

Literacy coaches provide job-embedded professional development to enhance teacher reflection, leading to better teacher decision making. Effective coaching attends to the characteristics of adult learners and promotes collaboration and reflection. Ultimately, literacy coaching, when done well, results in greater student achievement. Given these effects of coaching, it is easy to understand why coaching has become popular across the educational spectrum. To learn how to get these results from your coaching program, read on.

ADDITIONAL RESOURCES

Burkins, J.M. (2007). *Coaching for balance: How to meet the challenges of literacy coaching*. Newark, DE: International Reading Association.

Corrie, L. (1995). The structure and culture of staff collaboration: Managing meaning and opening doors. *Educational Review, 47*(1), 89–99. doi:10.1080/0013191950470107

Vogt, M., & Shearer, B.A. (2003). *Reading specialists in the real world: A sociocultural view*. Boston, MA: Allyn & Bacon.

CHAPTER 2

How Does Coaching Lead to Change?

- What should be the focus of my efforts to make changes in my school?
- Why is change so difficult?

Literacy coaches are in the change business. Their jobs wouldn't exist if someone didn't want something to change. Often, positions for literacy coaches are created because a school policymaker or administrator wants a coach to help teachers become more effective in implementing a program, raising test scores, or complying with new policies. Sometimes, literacy coaching is offered as a path to something more general, such as professional development or teacher effectiveness. In any event, with coaching comes the sense that something should change.

My goal with this chapter, then, is to help coaches think a bit about change. I hope coaches don't skip over this chapter, assuming that it will be abstract and impractical, because the ideas presented here about change can transform the way coaches conceptualize their work.

What Are You Trying to Change?

If literacy coaching is about change, then what are coaches trying to alter? Some literacy coaches help teachers implement a new reading program. Some literacy coaches work with new teachers to help them get a good start. Some literacy coaches focus on instructional strategies that increase test scores. Some literacy coaches are trying to change the way an entire school staff does its work. And many literacy coaches are expected to do all the previously mentioned tasks plus more!

In this section, I review the three areas on which literacy coaches might focus their change efforts: teachers' behaviors, teachers' attitudes, or teachers' thinking. This will clarify what's possible and what may be expected from literacy coaches and will also assist literacy coaches to start thinking about the approaches that they will use in their coaching work. Interestingly, I have found that the distinguishing characteristic among models of coaching is just this: What is it trying to change (Toll, 2007)? Thus, understanding the possible focuses of change in literacy coaching will help coaches select the model of coaching that makes the most sense to them and their schools.

Change Focused on Behavior

Some change efforts emphasize the behavior of participants. These efforts make explicit the behaviors that are desired and the method that will be used to gauge such behaviors. Traditional supervision models often have used behavior-focused approaches. For example, a principal might state that he or she wants to see writing taught in every classroom. The gauge of change is whether the appropriate behavior—in this case, teaching writing—can be observed when the principal visits the classrooms.

When a change in behavior is the goal, literacy coaches will want to make clear the following points:

- The desired behavior(s) (e.g., teachers will use running records)
- How the desired behavior(s) will look and/or sound in a classroom, or the frequency of the behavior (e.g., a running record will be recorded during an individual conference for each student at least monthly)
- How the behavior will improve student achievement (e.g., the running record will guide teachers in providing instruction targeted at students' instructional needs)

A limitation of behavior-focused coaching is that behaviors by themselves are often inadequate for bringing about significant changes. This kind of coaching may help teachers tweak a practice or develop additional instructional strategies, but without shifts in beliefs or understanding, new practices by themselves usually have limited effects.

Change Focused on Attitude

Coaching that focuses on teachers' attitudes is sometimes superficial—for instance, offering fun professional development workshops or providing a listening ear when teachers need to complain. There is nothing inherently wrong with doing either of these, but they are not going to lead to much of a change for students.

Yet, sometimes when the focus is attitude, coaches attempt to change beliefs, values, or perspectives in a challenging or intrusive manner. There is a difference between an attitude toward, say, a particular textbook that a teacher dislikes, and beliefs, values, or perspectives about teaching, learning, or students. The latter evolve slowly and are likely very significant to educators' professional identities; coaches are wise to be cautious in trying to change them.

The best example of a successful coaching endeavor that focuses on attitude is the Concerns-Based Adoption Model (CBAM; Hord, Rutherford, Huling-Austin, & Hall, 1987). The goal with CBAM is not to change attitudes but to *understand* participants' attitudes toward a proposed innovation to respond in the most helpful manner. The levels of concern in the CBAM are enumerated. Each of the following levels is described by an individual's stance toward a proposed innovation:

- *Level 0:* The teacher knows nothing about the innovation.
- *Level 1:* The teacher is collecting information to learn about the innovation.
- *Level 2:* The teacher is wondering how the innovation will affect her personally—will she have enough time, will it sap her energy, and other questions.
- *Level 3:* The teacher is trying to address practical issues raised by the innovation—fitting it in the schedule, managing the materials, and other issues.
- *Level 4:* The teacher is determining the effect—positive, negative, or nonexistent—that the innovation is having on her goals, particularly student achievement.
- *Level 5:* The teacher is interested in elaborating on the innovation, making modifications and fitting it into other goals or programs, and sometimes sharing ideas with others.
- *Level 6:* The teacher is satisfied with the innovation and interested in moving on to new problems and questions, perhaps those that are raised by the innovation itself.

A coach who is familiar with CBAM might notice the attitudes of teachers when presented, say, with close reading as a new component of the literacy program. Is a teacher saying that she isn't interested (level 1), asking questions about where to fit it into her already crowded day (level 3), or excited about sharing how she's already implementing close reading instruction (level 5)? The literacy coach would respond differently to each level of concern. For instance, if a teacher had no interest in close reading, the literacy coach might listen for an opportunity to suggest instruction in close reading as an option and to explain why it might be useful. However, if a teacher is concerned about fitting close reading instruction into her already crowded day, the literacy coach might ask if they could look at the teacher's daily schedule to work together to find a place for it.

Change Focused on Cognition

The emphasis of some coaching endeavors is teachers' thinking and understanding. These efforts support participants in deepening their thinking through reflection on students, including data about student learning as well as the content of instruction and good pedagogy. This reflection leads to better decisions about instruction, instructional materials, classroom arrangements, and the myriad other conditions of teaching and learning.

When teachers discuss significant matters in professional learning teams, they often experience challenges to their understanding. For instance, when a science teacher tells about success in using reading strategies to help students learn more about biology, a colleague on his team may be confused because she assumed those strategies were a waste of time. An effective literacy coach can help these teachers not only share practices but also share understandings about matters such as why students struggle when reading the textbook, why reading strategies are—or aren't—helpful, and how teachers might fit strategy instruction into a busy class period. Such conversations are essential if this team's work is to be transformative for all involved.

Choosing a Focus

Readers may wonder which approach to change is best for coaching: coaching focused on behavior, coaching focused on attitude, or coaching focused on thinking. In developing my AIM model of professional learning (Toll, 2012), I found that learning in one area affects learning in the others. For instance, if a middle school social studies teacher understands something new about how academic vocabulary is acquired, she may develop a new way to help English learners overcome the vocabulary challenges of civics. On the other hand, if a new teaching strategy enables that teacher to see greater success among students who are English learners, that new teaching behavior may lead to a shift in her beliefs about the ability of English learners to succeed in high school. Learning in one area affects a teacher's learning in another.

A second insight from my research into teacher professional learning is that learning focused on behavior often does not last. For instance, when teachers go to a workshop that provides a list of graphic organizers for writing instruction but get little help in understanding the writing process and do not gain perspective on how "real" writers write, those graphic organizers will not lead to significant changes in student success and in fact are likely to end up at the bottom of a file drawer, ignored. I'm not criticizing graphic organizers here; rather, I am suggesting that teachers need more than instructional activities if deep changes are sought.

However, when teachers take the time to understand an instructional process, a challenge in student learning, or some other aspect of the complex acts of teaching, learning, and literacy, they will likely make changes in their practices as well, but those changes will be rooted in knowledge and reflection. It takes more work to develop understanding than to adopt a new practice. For instance, teachers who have participated in National Writing Conference communities typically have taken weeks-long summer workshops supplemented with ongoing collaborative sessions throughout the school year; it takes time to understand the writing process and how teachers can support their students' growth as writers. The benefit, though, is that when teachers implement new practices—and programs such as the National Writing Project do indeed support new behaviors as well as new understandings—they do so with greater insight into why they would use a particular practice, and with which students, and for which outcomes.

The coaching conversation presented in Chapter 6, which I recommend as the crux of your coaching practice, is based in part on the insights presented here. It provides a protocol for coaches and their teacher partners to use in thinking about challenges and interests and then deciding to try something new as a result. Stay tuned!

Changing Our Understanding of Change

Conventional wisdom in education is as follows: Change is difficult and painful. Some teachers want to change and readily do so, but many resist and make life miserable for all of those who want to move ahead. It is important to plan for change and then implement the plan in a step-by-step manner until the change is completed. Change depends on one or more change agents who create the vision and support educators in doing what wouldn't get done otherwise.

These statements may be accurate in some instances, but in many instances, they aren't. What's more, the assumptions behind such statements—for instance, that there are "good" and "bad" teachers, change is something many resist, change has a discrete beginning and end, and a change agent "creates" change—are frequently harmful and lead to stereotypes. Often, literacy coaches with whom I work make mistakes because they are operating under these assumptions. By buying into conventional wisdom about change, some literacy coaches approach their work with unnecessary negativity and fear, and they—and the teachers with whom they work—make assumptions about the literacy coaches' roles and the beliefs about teachers on which the literacy coaches are basing their work.

I'd like to provide a few more insights into the change process to dispel some myths about change and to give coaches perspectives on what they are—and aren't—trying to do. I offer three points to help coaches in their work: Change is constant, change is different in every situation, and change is supported by relationships.

Change Is Constant

I went back to graduate school after trying to bring about change in several settings and in several roles. While working on my doctorate, I read everything I could get my hands on that had to do with change. I was particularly looking for an understanding of why some teachers change and others don't. I figured that if we could just understand that, we'd have the magic pill for educational change.

Meanwhile, I was trying to survive as a graduate student, so I occasionally took care of other parts of my life, including my spiritual self. I liked to read books on a range of spiritual perspectives, and one evening I was reading *It's Easier Than You Think: The Buddhist Way to Happiness* (Boorstein, 1995). This book is about Boorstein's understanding of how to live life from a Buddhist perspective.

At one point, I found myself nodding in agreement as I read Boorstein's statement that we are all constantly changing, that life flows like a river and we with it. Suddenly, it occurred to me that this contradicted the work that I was doing in my studies. In my professional life, I was looking for forces that start and stop change, but in my personal life, I was viewing change as the constant flow of life. This was a significant moment in my understanding of change.

After all, when you think of it, can you name one moment in your life when change has not taken place? Of course not. Every second, you are growing older, your cells are replacing themselves, your senses are taking in new information, and the air and people and world around you are revolving and altering. No moment is ever like the one before nor the one after. Yet, in schools we conceptualize change as an event, a one-time thing. For instance, we think that teachers learn how to engage students in shared reading and then can move on to the next problem. Not only does this interfere with our approach to change itself, but it also adds to our frustration because it leaves us with the sense that change, if done right, will take place once and then be finished. Then we feel like failures if one change takes place and it leads to the need for another and another and another.

What is different if we think about change as constant? First, we no longer look for starts and stops to change. Change does not become an event; it becomes a normal part of everyday life in school. Think about it: When we are advocating for a particular change, we often act as though that change is the only change we'll ever need. If someone stopped and asked us, we'd say that that isn't the case, of course, but unless we really do stop and think about it, we often proceed as though the change is the be-all and end-all. For instance, when a literacy coach is trying to convince teachers to implement writers' workshop, that implementation may become the focus of the literacy coach's goals. The literacy coach may lose sight of the fact that implementing writers' workshop, wonderful as the idea may be, is one change in an ongoing stream of changes. Without this perspective, the literacy coach risks becoming a missionary rather than a coach. Yet, if the coach recognizes that changes in writing instruction are going to be constant and thinks of him- or herself as one who influences those changes by advocating for writers' workshop, he or she will try hard, but not obsessively, to meet this goal.

The perspective that change is constant also leads one to recognize that change is part of everyone's life, even the lives of those teachers who appear resistant to change. At this point, you may be thinking about the teacher who seems stuck and never appears to change. I thought of that kind of teacher, too, when I started to think about change as ongoing for all of us. In particular, I thought about Bob (pseudonym). He was a teacher with whom I had worked for several years, and to me he looked pretty stuck. For instance, every year he did the same group activity for his social studies unit on Egypt. His sixth-grade students made a pyramid from cardboard boxes, and it took them weeks to get the project done. Every year, I pondered what instructional purpose the cardboard pyramid served, and every year I concluded that it had very little instructional value. Yet, Bob did the same thing, over and over. I once thought to myself that I wouldn't need a calendar if I knew which unit Bob was doing in his classroom; he followed the exact routine and schedule every year, it seemed to me.

One day, Bob came to see me to ask if I knew anything about when the school district might act on rumored plans to move sixth-grade classes from the elementary schools to the middle schools. "You see," Bob explained, "I'm concerned that if it doesn't happen soon, I might not have the energy to do it. Right now, I change easily, but in a few years, I'll be close to retirement, and that might be tough on me." I was stunned. Bob thought he changed easily!

A few years later, when I was thinking about these matters in graduate school, I thought about Bob with a wider perspective, and here's what occurred to me: At the time of our conversation about middle school, Bob had just seen his only daughter off to college. In addition, he had just dealt with the death of a relative who had been living in his home. Bob had a great deal of change going on in his life; it just wasn't easily visible at work.

I have concluded that individuals change at their own rates, and those who don't seem to be changing are probably just doing it in a way that is not easily perceived. The changes may be internal or taking place in a different setting, or perhaps these individuals change at a pace that makes it hard to see the changes unless they are observed over a long period of time.

If change is always happening, though, then school leaders, including literacy coaches, don't have to try to be change agents in the sense that they create change. Change is already happening and will continue without assistance. Rather, we may serve to direct, focus, speed up, or even slow down changes that are occurring. Think of sunshine coming through a magnifying glass. We can't control the sun, but we can focus its rays. In a similar manner, literacy coaches can provide resources, demonstrations, workshops, and conversations that lead and support the changes taking place.

One final insight that results from this new view of change is that, given that change is ongoing and everywhere, it is not totally in our control, and we'll only frustrate ourselves and others if we try to make it so. Again, I think of a metaphor, this time a rosebush. If I decide to plant a rosebush in my yard, I may have an image of what I want it to look like. That image will probably include perfectly shaped and colored roses, evenly spaced and regularly blooming on a shrub that is a certain height and perfectly fills a space in my yard. However, I will probably never achieve that exact rose bush, and if I do, it won't last. The forces of rain, wind, sunshine, drought, my forgetfulness, neighborhood children and dogs, and so on will prevent the bush from being perfect. It doesn't hurt me to have an idea in my mind of the rosebush I want: The vision will encourage me to tend to the rosebush and do my best to change it into that vision. But I'll be frustrated and perhaps even harm the bush if I become overly committed to making that perfect vision a reality.

The same idea is true for literacy instruction and programs. As a literacy coach, you might have a vision of what a good program looks and sounds like. In fact, I hope you do, and I encourage you to develop one if you don't. However, given the constant forces that will influence your attempts to get there, and the forces that will continue to act even if you do get there, you're doomed to frustration and failure if you hold too tightly to that vision. Change is ongoing in schools, and you can't rein it in to make it yours. Even if you accomplish what you aimed for, the constancy of change means that it, too, will pass.

Change Is Situated

A question was posed recently on a listserv for teacher educators. The author asked, "What would it take to 'fix' public education?" My response to this question is that first, we need to stop asking it. The question implies that there is one way to make schools better, and I believe this one-size-fits-all mentality is part of the problem. Those of you who have been educators for a while have seen it happen over and over again: Every few years, we learn of the next new thing that purportedly will save us all. However, within a few years (or occasionally, a few months), the new thing dies out and is replaced with something else, leaving in its wake the sense that the old innovation was mistakenly labeled a good idea and now we need to move on to the one that really is.

If you've been in education awhile, you also know that many of the innovations that came and went had merit. I'd suggest that the reason they didn't last is because we think of change as something that is universally the same. In other words, if an innovation is valuable, it has to work everywhere. Actually, Cuban (1998) has found that teachers don't think this way. Teachers generally believe that an innovation has value if it is flexible enough to be adapted to a variety of settings. Cuban found, though, that others—policymakers and the public, for instance—think the opposite. To them, an innovation is valuable if it can be implemented consistently across settings and yield consistent results across those settings, and of course, educators are vastly outnumbered by the general public.

Teachers are practical people who base a lot of their learning on action research, even though they don't always label it as such. If they see a problem in their classroom, they make some changes, and then they see if those changes are effective. This is the crux of action research. Among the things that teachers learn from their action research is that many innovations work with some classes and not with others, work with some students and not others, or work for some teachers and not others.

A good example of such an innovation would be literacy centers. I work with some teachers who love having literacy centers in their classrooms and couldn't imagine a readers' workshop without them. Other teachers find literacy centers to be overwhelming for them and their students and prefer to have students read and journal during the part of readers' workshop when the teachers might otherwise engage students in literacy centers. And some of these teachers change their opinions from year to year based on their classrooms, the level of additional support they have (resource teachers, student teachers, etc.), and their own energy levels.

However, those who write about readers' workshop may make claims that it always includes literacy centers or always includes silent reading and journaling. Teachers who want to change their literacy instruction may believe that they must include one or the other; therefore, some teachers will be successful, and others won't.

If educators think about change as situated—meaning that it depends on myriad shifting factors—the number of teachers succeeding at their attempted changes will increase. What's more, if educators remember that changes need adjustments in each situation and over time, the changes that are made are more likely to continue to lead to success.

Change Occurs When One Is Safe or Traumatized

It seems as though there is no middle ground for change. It occurs in safe environments and in unsafe ones. For example, I love to bicycle, and a few years ago, I decided to train for a six-day, 540-mile bike ride from St. Paul, Minnesota, to Chicago, Illinois, to raise money for AIDS charities. I had never done anything like this, and I spent months in training. One of the best sources of support that I had was a listserv of other riders, some of whom were new to that kind of riding, just like me, and some of whom had previously done rides like the one for which I was preparing. One of my concerns was how I would manage on the hilly portions of the route because the area of central Illinois in which I lived then is flat. I posted a question to the listserv and got great advice from someone who called himself Carbon Lord (the highest quality and fastest bicycles are made of carbon). He gave me detailed advice on how to manage hills, which enabled me to make it up all the hills on the ride. There were 1,700 bicyclists on that six-day ride, so I never caught up with Carbon Lord, but I learned at the end of the week that he had finished first every single day of the ride. Clearly, this guy was a master, yet his friendly and encouraging suggestions had still enabled me to learn from him and change significantly as a rider.

Another force that also changed me as a rider was a resident of a county road outside my town. This resident was a big dog. On one of my first training rides, the dog appeared suddenly beside me and, probably responding to some border collie genes in him, attempted to herd me with his body. I was knocked off my bike and had injuries serious enough to send me to the emergency room. I changed a lot as a rider because of this traumatic event. I never ride in the country without spray to ward off aggressive dogs; I have learned to make my voice strong in yelling, "No," or "Stay," to dogs running after me; and I have learned to watch for dogs as I approach every farm along the way.

My bicycle training exemplifies the two ways that most of us experience change: as part of a supportive relationship or as the result of trauma. Have you ever changed significantly in any other way?

I believe this is why supervisors have a hard time getting people to change. Traditional supervisory methods, such as goal setting, classroom observations, monitoring for fidelity, and plans of improvement, are often ineffective. They provoke stress, a condition under which most workers become less effective. Although they may produce superficial changes, they don't produce long-term changes because they are neither sufficiently supportive nor sufficiently traumatic.

For example, principal Beth Jones may develop an improvement plan with teacher Donna Smith in which Donna will post a word wall in her room. Donna may create the word wall but then only draw students' attention to it when Beth is in the room. This isn't much of a change. Acting as a supervisor, Beth's only real means of assuring change may be to traumatize Donna. If Beth's commitment to demanding change is strong enough, she may place Donna on a plan of assistance, demand that Donna change grades or buildings, or threaten to fire Donna.

At this point, you may be thinking, Wait a minute! That's not fair! There are many effective principals who support teacher change! I agree. But I don't believe they do it by acting as supervisors. As supervisors, they'll achieve change only by creating an upheaval, causing individuals, groups, or entire staffs to feel traumatized. Rather, the principals who are most effective in supporting change do just that—they support it.

Supporting change is different from acting like the boss and demanding it. When a teacher is supported in making changes, the environment is safe. He or she can try things, take chances, and make mistakes. A key to a supportive environment is supportive relationships with others. Although nature or pets can indeed make us feel supported, making significant change usually requires supportive relationships with humans.

As for traumatic change, it can be effective. If you've had a car accident while making a left turn at a corner, you probably have changed into a driver who is careful when making left turns. If you had a spouse or partner suddenly leave you, you probably have become more cautious about relationships with significant others. Although these kinds of traumas induce change, they come with a high price. Who would seek a car accident or a divorce for the sake of personal growth? For school leaders, including literacy coaches, the cost of traumatic change can include severed professional relationships, negative reputations that can't be overcome, and an inability to establish trust in the future. The change is rarely worth the cost.

Nonetheless, there are those who think change should be demanded of teachers. Currently, the demands for change are coming in the form of demands for improved test scores. For some educators, these demands are traumatic: Many teachers are burning out, feeling more powerless than ever before in their careers, and looking toward retirement or career changes. For other educators, these demands are not yet traumatic, probably because these teachers work in schools that had stronger test scores to begin with, but that is changing over time as the demands increase.

I encourage you to think about change as occurring in the context of a safe, supportive environment. It's the only way to achieve true growth—in other words, change that is significant and affirming.

Changing Change

I hope you consider the ideas that I just presented about change. You don't have to agree with them right away, but think about them for a while and see how you feel. First, you might think about how they describe changes outside your work experience. Do they fit the way you have changed in your relationship to your spouse or partner, in patterns at your place of worship, or in the manner by which you eat and exercise? In other words, do these ideas support or explain efforts to change in other parts of your life?

Literacy coaches may find that changed perspectives on change will alter the way they work. When they recognize that change is ongoing for their teacher partners, literacy coaches may stop mentally dividing their colleagues into two groups: those who change and those who don't. When they see the unique qualities of their schools and seek flexibility in bringing initiatives to life in a variety of settings, they may experience less frustration that everyone is not on the same page. When coaches recognize that the quality of their relationships may be the strongest factor in whether they make a difference in their school, they may engage even more sincerely with every teacher they work with.

Conclusion

Change occurs all the time in human lives. Unless one is dead, one is changing, however subtly. Therefore, change is not inherently difficult; some changes are a delight, and others are exceedingly hard. The difference is often how much control a person has over a change and how much support from others a person has while making a change.

Savvy literacy coaches reflect on the changes they wish to influence and their role in school change. They support teachers through the coaching conversation to identify significant problems or interests about which teachers learn deeply, reflect, and then try new practices to make a difference.

ADDITIONAL RESOURCES

Hord, S.M., Rutherford, W.L., Huling-Austin, L., & Hall, G.E. (1987). *Taking charge of change*. Alexandria, VA: Association for Supervision and Curriculum Development.

Sarason, S.B. (1996). *Revisiting "The culture of the school and the problem of change."* New York, NY: Teachers College Press.

Tyack, D., & Cuban, L. (1995). *Tinkering toward utopia: A century of public school reform*. Cambridge, MA: Harvard University Press.

Wheatley, M.J., & Kellner-Rogers, M. (1999). *A simpler way*. San Francisco, CA: Berrett-Koehler.

CHAPTER 3

How Do I Influence Teachers?

- What tasks should I spend my time on if I am to be most influential?
- Why don't teachers use the information I give them?
- What do I do when working with grade levels or content disciplines that I haven't taught?
- Why don't teachers appreciate my efforts?

Chapter 2 established that coaches are in the change business. This role in bringing about teacher change is best described as coaches' *influence*. Coaches don't demand or coerce change; rather, coaches partner with teachers as they solve problems and pursue interests that will enhance their students' learning, and by providing a trusting relationship, process skills, and a few ideas and resources, coaches support teachers in transformative work.

I like the last sentence as a summary of what effective coaches aim to do. If you do, too, then read on because in this chapter I provide a list of tasks that bring coaches' work to life, a suggested ratio for how much time should be spent on each task, and some perspectives on how to optimize your influence. These tools should help you be the influential coach you want to be.

Coaching Tasks

Literacy coaches influence teachers primarily through conversations that matter. These coaching conversations provide support for teachers' problem solving and pursuit of interests that will make a difference in their students' learning. In addition, coaching conversations follow a protocol that teachers can use to be systematic in addressing matters of importance, and they offer just enough nudge—that is, enough encouragement to persist—to create a cycle of continuous improvement. Chapter 5 is devoted to the coaching conversation.

Literacy coaches' influence also comes forth during demonstration lessons. The key to effective demonstration lessons is to ensure that they grow out of coaching conversations. Many coaches have done the opposite and offered demonstration lessons out of the blue—say, by declaring that it is think-aloud month and that teachers are welcome to sign up for a demonstration of think-alouds—and then feel disappointed when few teachers sign up for those demos or when those who do sign up leave the classroom to check their mail during the coach's lesson. Conversely, demonstrations that grow out of coaching conversations will be ones that teachers are interested in observing and learning from.

The remaining tasks that coaches engage in are likely "setting the stage" tasks—that is, tasks that prepare coaches for conversations or demonstration lessons and thus are necessary but not actually coaching tasks. Additionally, coaches will occasionally find themselves providing service to the school, such as professional development workshops, or service to students, such as serving on RTI teams, which are not coaching duties per se but reflect the fact that in most workplaces, people help out wherever they can.

Time for Tasks

I encourage literacy coaches to spend 50% of their time in coaching conversations, whether with individuals or groups. This is a big commitment, but the coaching conversation is that important. Coaches will want to reserve at least 20% of their time for demonstration lessons and 10% for setting the stage. This leaves 20% for those duties that I label service to the school and service to students. These proportions are illustrated in Figure 1.

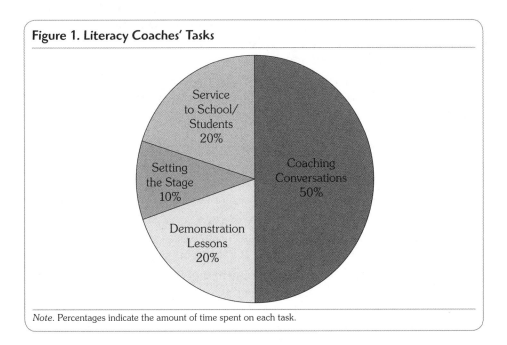

Figure 1. Literacy Coaches' Tasks

Service to School/Students 20%

Setting the Stage 10%

Coaching Conversations 50%

Demonstration Lessons 20%

Note. Percentages indicate the amount of time spent on each task.

For many coaches, this breakdown of how their time might be used is surprising because they use their time very differently. Often, the difference between what I suggest and how time is actually used reflects a different understanding of coaching. Sometimes it reflects the reality that a coach is unable to focus on his or her priorities because staff and administrators at the school have other expectations.

If you agree that time allocations will enhance your influence as a coach but you aren't yet there, then try to slowly make some changes. You don't have to declare overnight that you are going to spend 50% of your time in coaching conversations; rather, perhaps you will aim to go from having coaching conversations 10% of the time to 20% of the time. That would be the equivalent of going from one half-day each week for coaching conversations to the equivalent of one full day. Talk to your supervisor about intended changes and seek his or her help.

Observations?

You may notice that observing in classrooms is not on my list of tasks. I spend very little time observing in classrooms because such observations do not augment my coaching influence. Here are several reasons why:

- Showers and Joyce (1996) studied coach–teacher pairs in two groups. In one group, the partnership included coaches observing and giving feedback; in the other group, coaches did not observe and give feedback. Showers and Joyce found that the inclusion of observation and feedback did not influence the effectiveness of the coaching partnerships, so they decided to exclude it from their future work with coaching.

- The focus of classroom observation must be on teachers' behavior because an observer cannot objectively collect teachers' thoughts or feelings. However, experienced teachers' challenges are often related to nonobservable matters, such as their understanding of particular students or their reflection on data to make instructional decisions. Beginning teachers and a few other teachers who are struggling may benefit from observation, but for the majority of teachers, observation does not influence them greatly because it does not focus on the truly challenging aspects of an experienced teacher's work.

- No matter how much a coach declares otherwise, many teachers still feel that observations by coaches have the flavor of supervisory observations.

- Coaches who observe are often trying to find out what is "really" occurring in a classroom. Such coaches don't trust what teachers tell them and want to see for themselves. At minimum, this leads coaches to assume that their sensibilities are more accurate than teachers'. It may also lessen the trust between teachers and coaches and convey the sense that the coach is going to do the thinking for the partnership. True, everyone experiences situations differently, and teachers may indeed have different perceptions about their classrooms than coaches. However, coaches still need to start the coaching conversation with teachers' perceptions. Otherwise, coaches will need to get teachers to see things their way, either through selling or arguing their ideas, and this does not make for a good coaching relationship. With strong process skills and a good understanding of the coaching conversation, coaches will be able to help teachers use data and other information to accurately gauge what occurs in their classrooms, but those actions will come later as part of the coaching partnership.

- When coaches observe in classrooms and see something they would change, they often struggle to not raise the matter with teachers. To do so shifts the relationship from a coaching partnership to one in which one party is judging the other.

I *do* observe in classrooms when, as part of an ongoing coaching partnership that began with coaching conversations, not observations, a teacher partner and I decide that it might be helpful to have another set of eyes in the classroom. This is likely because the teacher is struggling to understand a particular student or implement a strategy that I demonstrated and that the teacher would like help in tweaking.

Now, I have found that this issue upsets coaches and administrators like no other. For many, observation is an inherent part of their coaching practice, and they can't imagine giving it up. I encourage coaches to reflect on the benefits of observations balanced with the drawbacks. Many coaches with whom I have worked have struggled initially to give up observing and then found, when they do, that it transforms their practice and greatly enhances their coaching collaborations.

Perspectives to Enhance Influence

I have noticed that some coaches, especially inexperienced ones, make assumptions about how their work makes a difference. Those assumptions often reflect coaches' idea that their job is to become really knowledgeable about all aspects of teachers' work and then gently pass that information on to their teacher partners to "get" teachers to change. Such approaches usually lead to frustration and ineffectiveness on the part of coaches. In the rest of this chapter, I provide perspectives that *will* be useful for coaches who want to make a difference.

It's Hardly Ever About Knowledge

Let me begin this section by telling you a story about my own coaching blunders. When I took on my first teacher leadership position, which included coach-like duties, I was one year out of graduate school. I had a master's degree in reading education, and I was confident in and proud of my new knowledge. My approach to the teachers with whom I was working reflected an unvoiced and unacknowledged (even to myself) belief that went something like this: If these teachers only knew what I know, then they'd be the kind of good teacher that I am.

I'm embarrassed to see the words I just wrote. It seems so disrespectful of the teachers with whom I was working, who probably had 250 combined years of teaching experience. However, in all honesty, it is what I believed. Needless to say, I didn't fare well in the coaching aspect of my job, although I must say that the teachers were quite kind to me in the manner in which they tolerated or ignored me.

I have found since then that the mistake I made is made by many literacy coaches. We think that the issue is knowledge, but it isn't. If knowledge were the essential component to change, then we'd all be very different. For instance, we'd all be slender. After all, we have knowledge that weight loss will result if we burn more calories than we consume. And we'd never speed on the highway, given that we know the speed limit and know the increased danger that speeding causes. I'm not claiming that knowledge doesn't matter—of course, it does—but knowledge alone does not lead to change.

You're probably nodding your head in agreement. Most educators understand the importance of attitudes, beliefs, and perceptions in assisting learners to learn; in other words, educators recognize that attitudes, beliefs, and perceptions can interfere with learners' abilities to acquire new knowledge. But that's not what I'm referring to here. I'm not saying that we have to consider attitudes, beliefs, and perceptions to help teachers put new knowledge to best use. I'm saying that the issue is rarely about knowledge in the first place. Consider the following examples:

Bob teaches fifth grade and never reads aloud to his class. He knows how to read aloud, and he has been told at workshops led by his district curriculum coordinator that reading aloud is a recommended instructional strategy for all elementary school teachers. However, Bob believes that it is a waste of time to read to fifth graders and that the kids would feel insulted if he read to them.

Melinda is a kindergarten teacher. She has read the summary of the National Reading Panel (NRP) report (National Institute of Child Health and Human Development, 2000), which recommends direct, systematic instruction in phonics for kindergarten teachers, and she knows that the NRP based its recommendation on a meta-analysis of research. However, Melinda has observed that some students in her classroom enter school with strong phonics knowledge because they have had frequent reading experiences at home, so she tries to replicate those home reading experiences instead of using the suggested phonics workbook. In addition, she finds teacher-generated research to be more useful than meta-analyses of experimental or quasi-experimental studies, so she pays little attention to the NRP's recommendations.

Sally's first-grade students are supposed to read for at least 15 minutes each evening, and an adult is to sign a form each week to indicate that this reading has been done. Sally knows that one of her students, Michael, spends his evenings with his grandmother while his mother works. Sally knows that the grandmother is fluent in reading and writing Spanish but not English. Michael indicates that he reads for more than 15 minutes each evening, and his knowledge of books would support this claim. However, he never returns the form because his grandmother cannot read it. Sally knows this is not Michael's fault, but she believes every student must be treated in the same manner and, therefore, gives him a "needs improvement" mark on his report card for the item "Completes Assignments." Also, when it is time for the quarterly movie and pizza party for those who have returned a signed form every week, Michael is excluded.

In each of these situations, knowledge is not the factor in the teacher's decision making. Rather, Bob's perceptions of middle school, Melinda's opinions about phonics learning and research, and Sally's value that all should be treated the same lead to the action that each educator takes.

Ironically, the preparation that most literacy coaches receive is in the knowledge domain. Currently, literacy coaches are taught about the five elements of instruction recommended by the NRP, instructional practices labeled "best," the Common Core State Standards, and perhaps the characteristics of effective professional development workshops. This kind of knowledge is helpful for literacy coaches, and I would not hire a coach who didn't have it. However, I find that knowledge is to coaching like a car is to driving. It's what propels the activity forward, but it won't happen successfully unless the person behind the wheel is skilled in steering it. A literacy coach who knows a great deal about literacy instruction but cannot develop relationships, build trust, and work with the non–knowledge-related issues of teaching will fail.

You're Not the Expert
New literacy coaches and those exploring the possibility of becoming literacy coaches often express to me their self-doubts, indicating that they don't think

they know everything they need to know to help teachers. (Again, issues of knowledge are at the forefront.) These individuals express concerns that they don't have as much teaching experience as the teachers with whom they might work, that they can't keep up with all the professional literature, or that they can't demonstrate expertise in all grade levels or content disciplines. In other words, they think they need to be experts to be good literacy coaches.

The notion of being an expert sets up literacy coaches for failure because no one can be an expert in all aspects of literacy teaching and at all grade levels. Moreover, even if literacy coaches were experts in all of those areas, it would be impossible for them to be experts in any particular teaching dilemma because such situations are unique to each teacher's classroom. Any group of students brings with it a unique set of characteristics, strengths, and challenges, plus a unique alchemy among the students themselves. Therefore, there is no way that literacy coaches could be experts on the students in every classroom.

Some literacy coaches are indeed experts, but only within a certain range of grades or on specific topics, such as close reading, writers' workshop, or disciplinary vocabulary. The people who have an easier time with literacy coaching are probably generalists: They know some things about most aspects of literacy teaching across a range of grade levels, but they are by no means experts in all of those things.

Trying to be the expert is damaging because, beyond trying to do the impossible, it interferes with the development of a trusting relationship with teachers. If literacy coaches present themselves as experts, teachers will respond either by believing or not believing that claim. Either response leads to problems for the coach, as described below:

- Teachers see the literacy coach as an expert. If teachers believe the literacy coach is an expert, then the literacy coach will fail to live up to their expectations because, again, no individual can be an expert in all aspects of teaching at all grade levels and with all groups of students. Meanwhile, the teachers who turn to the literacy coach as expert often fail to acknowledge their own expertise. In addition, believing in the literacy coach as an expert creates a sense that there is a discrete set of information (which brings us back to the knowledge myth again) that is essential for teaching successfully, and that the task is for teachers to take in that knowledge and make it their own. Such a notion obscures the fact that good teachers are problem finders and problem solvers, not possessors of all the expert knowledge that they will ever need.

- Teachers dispute the literacy coach's efforts to appear to be an expert. On the other hand, some teachers will not believe that the literacy coach is an expert. If the literacy coach maintains the stance of expert and teachers doubt it, communication will become a power struggle, with all the individuals involved trying to prove that they are right. Moreover, there is a risk that teachers who doubt the literacy coach's expertise will note every time the literacy coach is not all-knowing, and they may bring these moments to everyone's attention to gain power over the coach and/or the situation. Here's an example:

Betty and Beatrice, sixth-grade teachers, are sure that their literacy coach, Jorge, is not the expert that he claims to be. When at a faculty meeting he incorrectly states that the sixth-grade spelling lists are not correlated with the content areas, Betty and Beatrice exchange looks across the room. A week later, Betty asks Jorge about the latest research on writing revision, and Jorge stammers. Betty tells Beatrice about this at lunchtime, and they both note this failure on Jorge's part for future use. Finally, at a staff meeting to discuss a new writing program, Jorge inaccurately describes the state-mandated writing assessment. Beatrice uses this opportunity to prove that he is not an expert: She raises her hand and begins explaining why she doesn't think the program, which Jorge is advocating for, is a good idea. In the process, she points out Jorge's inaccurate claims about the state test and hints that he has not learned about the current sixth-grade program well enough. She also cites some research on writing instruction that contradicts Jorge's stammering response to Betty a few weeks earlier. Jorge looks uninformed, and his position as advocate for the writing program is undermined considerably. Betty and Beatrice have used their previous insights about his lack of expertise against him.

Some new literacy coaches worry that a nonexpert approach will backfire because it will lead teachers to assume that the literacy coach knows nothing and can't help them. To avoid this situation, you might want to practice a short explanation of how you see your role and the role of the teacher. When I'm getting to know teachers in a literacy coaching situation, I usually say something like this:

> I don't approach this job as an expert. Although I know some things, I also know that you know some things. We are all experts to an extent, and when we share our expertise, think how far we can go!

The goal is to make clear that your literacy coaching task is not about telling the teachers what you know and expecting them to accept it without question. Rather, the message should be that coaching is about relationships, sharing, and mutual respect for the purpose of helping one another grow.

True Respect

Educators frequently talk about respect: We respect one another, we respect our students, and we respect administrators. Literacy coaches express the same desire to be respectful. In my experience, though, what is referred to as respect often means being friendly and polite while manipulating others into doing what you want them to do.

For example, Moira is a literacy coach in an elementary school. She sees teachers assigning many activities in which students are asked to respond to what was read but are not helped to develop strategies for understanding. She wants the teachers at her school to provide instruction and practice in reading comprehension strategies, but she wants to be respectful. Here's her plan:

Moira knows that Kevin, a second-grade teacher, is successfully providing strategy instruction for reading comprehension, so she highlights his teaching at an after-school workshop. Then, when conferencing with Melinda, the other second-grade teacher, Moira offers to cover Melinda's class for a morning so Melinda can observe Kevin's strategy instruction. Meanwhile, Moira approaches the fourth-grade teachers, Patrice and LaWanda. They have taught together for 10 years and have established parallel routines. However, Moira and LaWanda are both interested in quilting, and Moira uses that opportunity to get to know LaWanda better. She learns that LaWanda wants to do an integrated unit with quilts as the theme, but Patrice is not interested. Moira suggests that she'll work with LaWanda on such a unit, and LaWanda agrees. Moira doesn't mention it to LaWanda, but she intends to incorporate reading comprehension strategy instruction into the unit. Moira has fewer ideas for how to approach the teachers in first and fifth grades, so she begins in a low-key manner by placing articles from *The Reading Teacher* in their mailboxes once a week, with a note that she'd be glad to talk about them if the teachers are interested. In addition, Moira knows that the teachers in grade 3, Holly and Chandra, are not providing the kind of instruction that she recommends. In fact, they have openly resisted Moira's suggestions and failed to attend the last two after-school workshops that she led. Therefore, Moira decides not to waste time on Holly and Chandra. Rather, she focuses on the teachers she believes she can move along most easily.

If asked, Moira would state unequivocally that she is respecting teachers. She would say that she is focusing on Kevin's success and enabling Melinda to have the opportunity to experience the same success. She would suggest that she is capitalizing on LaWanda's own interest and that her low-key approach to the teachers in the first and fifth grades is nonthreatening and not forcing them to change. As for Holly and Chandra, Moira would say that she is showing respect to them and the entire school by not causing trouble.

I feel a bit unkind in suggesting that Moira isn't being as respectful as she might be. Like many real-life literacy coaches, this imaginary literacy coach is trying her best to implement her notion of what respect looks and sounds like. Unfortunately, respect is one of those virtues that we all strive to practice but rarely discuss or get assistance in practicing. So, let's look at various examples of respect:

- There's the "respect" that junior high school kids want, which means, "You, the adult, are respecting me when you let me do whatever I want and then pick up the pieces when I make a mistake."
- There's the "respect" of an unhappily married couple, in which both partners loathe some of the other's habits but remain silent out of respect for the sanctity of the marriage.
- There's the "respect" of the doctor who fails to address her heart patient's smoking habits because she knows it will upset the patient.
- There's the "respect" of a police officer who politely tells a driver to have a good day after giving her a $75 speeding citation.
- There's the "respect" of an office worker who wants the desk near the window and, therefore, begins to tell his colleague, who has the window desk, about the harmful effects of the sun's rays.

These might seem like dubious examples of respect, but in some ways they parallel the respect that Moira is showing to the teachers in her school. She is deciding what is best for the teachers with whom she works and then developing strategies to get them to do what she wants. These strategies include the subtle manipulation of placing journal articles in mailboxes, encroaching on a 10-year teaching partnership when she sees an opportunity, and dismissing those teachers who don't agree with her. Moira's subtle manipulation is aimed at meeting her goals without considering the teachers' goals. I suggest that this is not true respect.

I also suggest that these approaches leave teachers feeling uncomfortable. Moira is naive if she thinks the teachers aren't aware of what is going on at some level. Most adults can sense when they are being manipulated, and none of us likes to feel this way. In fact, such a feeling reduces trust and is detrimental to relationships. In a truly respectful relationship, the parties involved strive for a balance between being themselves as much as possible and honoring the needs of others to be themselves as much as possible.

Table 2 demonstrates what respect in a literacy coaching relationship might look and sound like. As you can see, this approach is one in which the literacy coach is a listener and learner first. The purpose of this attentiveness to the teacher is to truly learn about the teacher and the work that he or she is doing. The literacy coach listens carefully and asks carefully worded questions that

Table 2. What Respectful Literacy Coaching Relationships Look and Sound Like

Objective	Looks Like	Sounds Like
Planning for coaching	The literacy coach meets with teachers to listen to and learn about their concerns, strengths, needs, and efforts so far.	"When you [the teacher] think about your goals for your teaching—the kind of readers and writers you want your students to be, the kind of classroom you want to have, and the kind of work you want to do—what gets in the way?"
Altering teaching practices	The literacy coach and teacher look at data, standards, curricular goals, student characteristics, and teaching strengths and interests in order to establish priorities.	"What are you doing successfully? What do you want to do differently? How can I help?"
Improving assessment practices	The literacy coach and teacher plan for assessment while planning for instruction and then collect meaningful data, including student work samples. Schoolwide, teachers examine and talk about a range of formal and informal assessments and what they mean for the curriculum, staff organization, and school goals.	"How will you know when your efforts have been successful? What will success look and sound like?"
Organizing for instruction	The literacy coach and teacher plot the teacher's daily and weekly schedules and match teaching goals to time allocations. This process includes consideration of how multiple goals and standards can be met with particular organizational structures and ways to collaborate with other school staff members.	"Let's find the time and human resources to make this possible."

indicate that he or she is there to help the teacher meet his or her goals, not the other way around. In such a truly respectful relationship, the teacher and literacy coach may not agree, but they have enough trust that they can express their goals, beliefs, and values without worrying that the other person will either dismiss or manipulate them.

Myles Horton, founder of the famous Highlander Folk School, expressed this concept by saying that a good education includes "respect for people's abilities to learn and to act and to shape their own lives" (Horton & Freire, 1990, p. 177). Just as Horton and his colleagues applied this concept to their education of adults seeking social change in the mid-1900s (including Rosa Parks), so can literacy coaches seeking educational change apply this concept of respect to their work. Literacy coaches do so when they recognize that teachers need to act and shape their own work lives. Respectful literacy coaches ask good questions, provide resources, make suggestions, assist in problem finding and solving, demonstrate instructional strategies, and engage in other activities to influence teachers' changes, but with an emphasis on the teachers' goals. In contrast, literacy coaches who lack true respect focus on getting teachers to implement the coaches' goals.

Conclusion

Literacy coaches optimize their influence when they are clear about the tasks that matter and when they monitor their time to ensure that they are mainly focused on those tasks. In addition, influential coaches truly respect their teacher partners and recognize that their own role is not to be the expert. Knowledge is important, but it is not the only component of effective coaching.

The next section of this book provides details for how to bring these perspectives to life by offering communication strategies, details of the coaching conversation, and tools for collaborating with teams.

ADDITIONAL RESOURCE

Lawrence-Lightfoot, S. (1999). *Respect: An exploration.* Reading, MA: Perseus.

What Does a Successful Literacy Coach Do?

CHAPTER 4

How Do I Begin My Work as a Literacy Coach?

- How can I make a good first impression?
- How do I approach the many kinds of teachers in the school?
- What's the best way to introduce myself to the principal, the staff, and the parents?
- What if my offers of help are met with silence?

First impressions count: We've all heard this adage, and many of us believe it to one extent or another. In education, first impressions do seem to matter. Think of the chatter among the teachers after the new principal conducts the first staff meeting or the effort that you have put into making a good impression with parents at back-to-school nights or open houses. As you might guess, it is equally important for literacy coaches to make good first impressions and to start off right. This chapter offers some tips for doing so.

Laying the Groundwork

It will be helpful for you to think about some things before you meet the people with whom you will be working. Here are some questions to ponder:

- Which of my personal qualities do I want the staff to notice from the start?
- How do I want my role to be understood? For instance, do I want to be seen as a change agent, support system, or resource? (If your response is "all of the above," then you might choose to prioritize these roles.)
- What is the likeliest negative response that I might initially receive from staff members, and what can I do to prepare for it?
- How can I describe my literacy coaching duties in a few words?
- How do I want to spend my first two weeks on the job?

Your responses to these questions can help you think about the manner in which you introduce yourself to staff members individually as well as in a group. In addition, they will help you develop language to use in explaining your work to others and may indicate some trouble spots for which you already can begin preparing.

Meeting the Principal

Sit down with the principal as early as possible and definitely before you meet the staff as a group. Prepare notes on the points that you want to make and the issues that you want to explore. I recommend that your list include the following items:

- The job description (Review it or plan for developing one if none exists.)
- Visions of literacy coaching—yours and the principal's
- History of coaching, professional development, and literacy instruction at the school (if you or the principal are new to the school)
- Your background and beliefs (Be brief and support your comments with your résumé or philosophy statement.)
- Communications with the principal—how often and in what format
- The importance of confidentiality (You want to build trust with the teachers and hope that the principal will stop you if you *ever* seem about to share information that will influence supervisory decisions.)
- First steps for meeting staff, students, and parents
- Priorities for the start of the year
- Your plans for individual and small-group meetings
- Available resources (time, money, staff)
- Next meeting time, location, and topics

Try to avoid gossiping about the staff or appearing interested in working with the principal to manipulate the staff. Demonstrate that you are professional in all aspects of the work you do.

Meeting the Staff

What do staff members want to learn from you when you first meet them? No doubt, some people are thrilled that you are there and can't wait to hear when you'll be available to assist them. I call these the Ready-to-Go Group. On the other end of the spectrum, other people probably dread your presence in the building and are attempting to determine how to avoid you or convince you to go somewhere else. I call these the Put-on-the-Brakes Group. The rest of the staff will be someplace in between, perhaps feeling curiosity, cautious enthusiasm, or restricted skepticism. I call these the Wait-and-See Group. The characteristics of these groups are outlined in Table 3.

Table 3. Staff Groups Encountered by New Literacy Coaches

Group	Characteristics	Challenges to Coaching	Tips for Working With This Group
Ready-to-Go	▪ Eager to try new things ▪ Enjoy working with colleagues ▪ Confident—not afraid to talk and ask about what they want to learn ▪ 10–20% of staff	▪ Can easily use up all of the coach's time ▪ May tempt the coach to focus too much on them because they are pleasant to work with ▪ Might intimidate coaches who lack confidence	▪ Give them the same amount of attention as other groups. ▪ Leverage this group's enthusiasm by asking them to help you try out practices that are new to you. ▪ Use teachers in this group as examples some of the time but not too often. ▪ Encourage members of this group to share their knowledge and skill with teachers in other schools.
Wait-and-See	▪ Eager to learn but cautious about changes ▪ Looking for quick signs of success (e.g., "OK, show me") ▪ May seek clarifications about roles and expectations ▪ 60–80% of staff	▪ May be thinking about past initiatives and wondering how literacy coaching is different ▪ May feel hesitant to stand out from the group in their teaching practices or environment ▪ May be overwhelmed by day-to-day concerns that prevent them from volunteering for new initiatives ▪ May be influenced by teachers who act as hubs	▪ Lead with the need: Identify and address immediate needs of these teachers to yield speedy results. ▪ Listen and learn about past efforts of these teachers; seek to identify ways that literacy coaching could be different. Ask the teachers for help. ▪ Encourage teachers to work in teams so they are not trying new things on their own.
Put-on-the-Brakes	▪ Want nothing to do with the literacy coach ▪ Feel satisfied with their work as it is or so dissatisfied that they don't want anyone to know ▪ May have a history of resisting initiatives ▪ 10–20% of staff	▪ Often exert influence over colleagues that discourages colleagues from participating in literacy coaching ▪ May be quite vocal ▪ May be intimidating to the literacy coach	▪ Do not avoid these teachers. ▪ Do not give these teachers undue time or mental energy. ▪ Support these teachers in an honest and authentic manner. ▪ Listen and learn about past experiences and current beliefs and practices of these teachers. ▪ Take your time but don't give up.

New literacy coaches sometimes make the mistake of focusing on one of the groups at either end of the spectrum. Some literacy coaches put their attention on the best-case scenario and speak to the entire staff as if they are ready to jump in and work together to create major changes. These literacy coaches sometimes demonstrate their affiliation with the Ready-to-Go Group by referring to accomplishments already achieved by this group that the coaches hope to build on. This approach will likely induce even more caution in the Wait-and-See Group and may cause the Put-on-the-Brakes Group to become defensive. Conversely, new literacy coaches sometimes focus on the Put-on-the-Brakes Group by speaking about the need to move slowly and the literacy coaches' interest in making everyone feel at ease. Well-intentioned coaches want even the most hesitant or resistant staff members to feel comfortable, so they may inadvertently convey that they are there to support the status quo, perhaps even to make the status quo easier to live with.

So, what tone would I suggest for literacy coaches meeting the staff for the first time? As you may have guessed, I advocate a middle-of-the-road approach. I think literacy coaches will make the most productive impressions if they honor the range of perspectives and practices that exist within most staffs. These literacy coaches will wisely avoid acknowledging particular practices or perspectives as the ones they find most exciting to work with. In addition, they will demonstrate enthusiasm for meeting the staff and interest in getting to know them but avoid overwhelming the hesitant staff members with the strength of their introductory comments.

Here is an example of one coach's middle-of-the-road introduction:

> Hi. I'd like to give you a sense of who I am and what I'm doing here. I'll give you all a copy of my job description, but in a nutshell, I'm here to help you help your students achieve in literacy and beyond. I'll soon be meeting with you as individuals and teams to discuss what that might look like in your particular instance. Meanwhile, what I want to say is that while I have my own strengths, I know you do, too. I hope we can work together to share one another's expertise. I believe my first job is to listen and learn—to get to know you, your interests, and your concerns. I believe we're all working for the success of the students at this school, and I look forward to being part of that effort.

An introduction such as this establishes that you want to focus on student success, that you honor your colleagues' knowledge and experience, that you are eager to get to know the staff members, and that you have a sense of what you're about.

Think of your first interactions with the school staff as the foundation for your future work together. Although poor starts can be repaired, strong starts give literacy coaches the advantage of making teachers excited about working with them.

Before moving on from consideration of teachers' range of readiness to work with coaches, I want to introduce the concept of hubs. Complexity scientists have pointed out that some people in groups act like hubs. To understand this concept, think of airport hubs. If you live in a smaller city or rural area and want to fly to a location across the country, you may have to take a regional flight from a smaller airport to a larger airport, or hub, from which many airlines have routes all over the country. For instance, if I want to fly just about any place from my home in Madison, Wisconsin, I take a regional jet to Chicago's O'Hare International Airport, which acts as a hub for many of the world's airlines. Many flights lead to O'Hare, and many flights depart from there.

Similar to an airport hub, some people act as hubs in that they receive and distribute a great deal of information. In schools, the hub-like teachers are the ones who are the first to know who is pregnant and who the new principal will be, what will happen at the staff meeting, and when the school board will act on a proposed initiative. These folks have a vast communication network and are trusted by others to be judicious in sharing what they know.

Sometimes literacy coaches are told to go with the goers—that is, to partner with those teachers who volunteer first and to take advantage of those teachers' excitement to get other teachers interested. However, the Ready-to-Go Group can sometimes consume all of a coach's time and may be perceived by others on the staff as the focus of the coaching initiative. In these cases, a "go with the goers" approach is not productive. On the other hand, if the goers are hubs, coaches' work with them will easily be conveyed to others, and those others will likely be influenced to partner with coaches as well.

How can a coach recognize a hub? Pay attention to who shares new and valuable information over lunch or at meetings, notice who influences opinions when a difficult decision is being made, and identify the most influential committee and note who chairs it. Details such as these will give you a pretty good sense of the hubs in your school.

Meeting Individuals and Small Groups

I encourage you to formally meet with individual staff members or in grade-level teams as soon as possible. You may be wondering which is better, individual or small-group meetings, and unfortunately, I can't say for sure. Often, this choice depends on schedules. In some schools, all teams meet at the same time, making it impossible for coaches to meet with more than one team each week. In other schools, teams meet according to varying schedules, and coaches can easily manage to see all of them. It is ideal to meet both with groups and with individuals early in the school year, but if that isn't possible, Table 4 may help you decide which way to go.

Table 4. Individual Versus Small-Group Introductions

Advantages	Disadvantages
Individual Introductions	
• You have more time to listen to each person. • An individual staff member may tell you something that he or she would not be comfortable sharing in a group. • You and the staff member have a greater opportunity to get to know each other as individuals. • The meetings are fairly easy to schedule because you only have to coordinate two schedules, yours and that of the staff member.	• Some individuals are more comfortable voicing potentially controversial perspectives if they know there are others in the group who share their views. • You don't have the contributions of additional perspectives, which is especially desirable if the individual with whom you are meeting is very negative or narrowly focused. • Individual meetings with all staff members take more time on your part.
Small-Group Introductions	
• If held with grade-level or department teams, including specialists and resource teachers, such meetings can build a sense of community. • You can get a sense for how teams do or don't work together. • Participants will learn how their colleagues feel about important matters. • Individuals who prefer not to speak up in a whole-staff meeting may feel comfortable speaking up at a small-group meeting and, therefore, will be heard by some of their colleagues. • It takes less time to meet with a handful of teams than with all teachers individually.	• One or two vocal participants can dominate the discussion. • A literacy coach without strong group facilitation skills might feel overwhelmed by a highly vocal group. • Team meetings sometimes are difficult to schedule because they require a shared planning time or a time outside the regular school day when all group members can meet.

You might ask your principal for advice or go to the staff and ask how they prefer to meet you initially. No matter which approach you use at the start of the year, include both individual and small-group meetings in your literacy coaching duties as the year continues.

The first face-to-face meeting with teachers, either individually or in small groups, is often the point when literacy coaches damage their positive first impressions. Here are some common mistakes to avoid:

In a grade-level meeting, the literacy coach asks the teachers what they'd like to do differently. The coach is met with silence.

These scenarios represent unintended blunders on the part of well-intentioned literacy coaches. What happens in each scenario is that the literacy coach makes an assumption about the teachers with whom he or she is working, and the teachers deliver a clear message that the assumption is wrong: They don't want to do things differently, they don't want the literacy coach's offer of help, and they definitely don't want to be observed in their classrooms by the literacy coach.

I don't want to stereotype all teachers with these scenarios. In most schools, there will be a few teachers who find such offers of help appealing, but most teachers won't. This seems to be just a reflection of human nature. After all, who wants to volunteer when someone shows up to provide unsolicited assistance? This approach to literacy coaching is sort of like selling merchandise door to door: The literacy coach shows up and tries to get a foot in the door by making an offer they can't refuse. Most people are pretty wary of such offers.

So, what should a literacy coach do? Frame the work ahead in terms of what teachers want to do for their students. In this way, a teacher doesn't feel singled out as in need of being "fixed." Rather, the teacher and literacy coach focus on how to help the students. Here's the start-up question that works well for me: "When you think about the reading and writing that you want your students to do and the teaching that you want to do, what gets in your way?"

I think this question (which I'll refer to as The Question from this point on) works because it avoids any implication that something is wrong with the teacher. In addition, although it makes an assumption, it makes one that is virtually always accurate: Teachers want their students to succeed and have an idea of what kind of learning and teaching will lead to that success. Various teachers may disagree about what those paths to success are or how they can gauge success, but they do want students to succeed. In addition, The Question focuses on the limitations to success "out there," not within the teacher. You might think this is naive (e.g., what if the teacher needs to change?), but I suggest that it is the only way you can develop trust and is an excellent way to start a conversation with a teacher. A statement that sums up this concept of acceptance before change is a well-known quote from Carl Rogers (1989): "The curious paradox is that when I accept myself as I am, then I change" (p. 17). I'll share more about The Question in Chapter 6.

Meeting Students

Literacy coaches are frequently in classrooms, so it is important that the students get to know them. I encourage you to ask classroom teachers for permission to read a book or an amusing article to their students in the first two weeks of the school year. By doing this, you will accomplish several things: First, the students will become familiar with you. This process will be helped if you say a few words about who you are and why you are working in the school before you read to the students. Second, you will provide one more reading experience for students. Third, you will get a feel for each class. Fourth, you will let the teachers get a feel for you. Finally, you will be of service at the start of the school year, when many teachers appreciate a few minutes' break to attend to beginning-of-the-year details.

I encourage you to make yourself visible and accessible to students throughout the school year as well. Attend assemblies, visit the lunchroom, and show an interest in the students. One strategy that has worked for me is to tell the students when I introduce myself that I would like to share a secret signal that they can use to indicate that they've been reading. I tell them that the secret signal is the thumbs-up sign, and when I see them in the hall or elsewhere, if they have been reading, they can quietly give me this signal. I make sure to make the signal back to the students as well. In this way, I communicate the expectation that reading is something that is a frequent activity and something to be proud of. This signal also gives the students a way to greet me without causing a lot of noise. Of course, this practice would probably seem silly to older students. As an alternative, you might merely engage middle school or high school readers in informal conversations about what they've been reading. To create such conversations, you might routinely chat with students in the lunchroom or hallways. Carrying an interesting book that appeals to that age group is a good way to begin such discussions.

Literacy coaches are typically very comfortable interacting with students. However, as they become busy in their work with teachers, coaches may struggle to find time to interact meaningfully with students. Moreover, if the coach is new to the building, the students may not recognize the literacy coach when they see him or her. By introducing yourself to students at the beginning of the year, you will begin to get to know the students and start to develop routines that will enable ongoing interaction throughout the school year.

Meeting the Parents

When you are new to a school, be sure to introduce yourself to parents. You may think of this as a lower priority task; however, literacy coaches need parents' support and have expertise to share with parents. Moreover, a growing body of research is demonstrating the value of bridging children's home and school literacies. If you as a literacy coach want to engage in such an effort, you will be wise to get to know the parents at your school and the literacies that they possess.

There are easy ways to introduce yourself to parents, such as a note in a school newsletter or on the school's website or an appearance at a meeting of the parent–teacher group. I encourage you to go beyond these steps, though, to create opportunities for meaningful interaction with as many parents as possible. For example, if you work at an elementary school, offer evening read-a-thons in which families rotate to four stations over a two-hour period. These stations might include a guest reader station (featuring the principal, the mayor, area sports figures, and local celebrities), a silent reading station (where families explore a room full of poetry in books, handouts, and posters), and a buddy reading station (at which kids read with one another, and the adults have a short session with you).

Another way to introduce yourself to parents is to arrange a special reading-related program for each grade level. The event might include opportunities for students to read their own writing to their parents or to perform a play based on a book that they read. Those in attendance might receive a take-home writing kit or engage in a "make your own bookmark" art activity. When the event includes students and enables them to have fun, they are motivated to attend and will encourage their parents to be there.

Coaches who work with high school students likely realize that these suggestions work better with younger kids. To connect with parents of high schoolers, coaches might offer student–parent sessions on study skills or preparing for college entrance exams.

These are just a few ideas for making yourself visible and accessible to parents. Wise coaches will develop two or three strategies that they'll regularly use to help them connect with parents.

If You Were Previously Part of the Staff

Some coaches find that their jobs are easier if they taught in their school before becoming a coach, whereas others find that familiarity with the school and its staff leads to special challenges. The latter often occurs because of the existing affiliations that coaches have established with some staff members but not others or because, as teachers in the building, coaches provided the staff with at least some idea of what they believe about literacy, teaching, and learning. These are not bad things to do. Whether you are a literacy coach or a classroom teacher, you are entitled to have close colleagues and to have beliefs and preferences. However, as a new literacy coach who previously taught at the same school, you are not really new. In other words, many staff members probably have formed opinions of you already.

My best advice is to be consistent and honest. As far as consistency goes, continue to be the person that you have been. Don't suddenly change your views or become cool to your on-staff friends. This will lead to distrust of you among many staff members. As for honesty, speak up when you are in a situation in which you have previously voiced an opinion other than the group's or other than the one you now must consider as a literacy coach and instructional leader.

For example, let's say that you've been vocal about the need for students to have access to materials that are not leveled when they are reading for pleasure, inquiry, or in the content areas. (This is in opposition to the thinking that students should always read at what is perceived to be their grade level.) If the staff is discussing the value and use of leveled books, don't pretend to be neutral on the subject. Instead, acknowledge your previously aired views and then affirm your interest in hearing and considering others' views as well. You might say the following:

> As many of you know, I've been vocal in my support of students reading nonleveled books during parts of the day. I know that some of you agree with that position and that some of you don't. My job now is not to make sure that my viewpoint wins but to make sure that we use an effective process for dealing with this disagreement. I promise to do my best to be a fair leader and consider all perspectives on this issue.

Then, do exactly what you said!

Repairing a Poor Start

Don't panic if you already have started your literacy coaching job and have not had a smooth beginning. The Buddhist teacher Pema Chödrön (1997) says, "Everything is workable" (p. 206), and I think that applies here. You can still apply the ideas in this book. However, if they contradict what you've said or done previously, you need to be open about that discrepancy. Admit that you started out thinking differently and have decided that another approach might be better. It can be difficult to admit that you've made mistakes, and it can be humbling to ask your colleagues to give you another try. But think about it: Your job will only get more difficult if you continue down a path that is ineffective. In addition, mature individuals on the staff will respect you for your willingness to reflect on your actions and continue growing. In fact, isn't that what you are hoping the teachers will do themselves?

Conclusion

A good start will serve you well as a literacy coach. It will help you establish yourself as a positive, likable, and trustworthy individual. Moreover, it will give others a sense of why you are there and what you hope to do in your job. It is an investment in the rest of the school year (and beyond) because it gives you a solid starting point of mutual respect and openness, as well as a sense of direction. This strong start, like all work of literacy coaches, requires good communication skills. The following chapter will help you enhance the effectiveness of your communication.

ADDITIONAL RESOURCE

Hallowell, E.M. (1999). *Connect: 12 vital ties that open your heart, lengthen your life, and deepen your soul.* New York, NY: Pocket.

CHAPTER 5

How Can I Communicate Well?

- What are key communication strategies for literacy coaching?
- How can I be a good listener?
- How can I be responsive to teachers without being too directive?
- How can I encourage teachers to open up to me?

A good deal of the work done by literacy coaches is verbal, and much of that work is done in conversation. Literacy coaches meet routinely with teachers, principals, teaching assistants, students, and parents. The discussions usually are not about the literacy coaches' own work, and when discussing others' work, the potential pitfalls are many. No one likes to feel judged, labeled, or put down. Even positive statements made by a literacy coach can be misunderstood by others, leading those who hear such comments to wonder whether a particular coach thinks he or she is superior to them.

Wise literacy coaches develop communication skills that minimize the chances that their words will be misunderstood or misinterpreted and that maximize trust and communication between themselves and those with whom they work. This chapter provides strategies that are useful in these endeavors. The first strategy is listening; second, I offer general tactics for coaching communications; and finally, I suggest words and phrases that are particularly helpful. You may want to make a bookmark or index card with these tips on it and attach it to your tablet, laptop, or some other place where you'll see it easily. However, good communication doesn't come from memorizing a list of strategies. These tips are only scaffolds to assist you as you practice the coaching skills of listening, prompting, and responding and as you discover your own words to value in your coaching work.

Listening

Listening is just a matter of using one's ears, right? This is the basis of listening, but despite the simplicity of the process, its success rate is not that high. People fail to really hear what others are saying all the time. The International Listening Association states that "'listening is the process of receiving, constructing meaning from, and responding to spoken and/or nonverbal messages'" (as quoted by Wolvin, 2010, p. 9). Let's look at these three stages of listening in action.

At the end of the day, your spouse tells you that he is exhausted from the day at work. To successfully listen to him, you do the following:

1. You receive his message by taking in the words with your ears ("Whew, what a day!") as well as by hearing your spouse's tone of voice and seeing the way he drops his jacket wearily on the couch.

2. You make sense of your spouse's words and actions to conclude that he is tired because the workday has been long, difficult, or both. You know this even though he didn't actually say it. (Also note that if he had said "Whew, what a day!" but done something else, such as rub his hands together and smile broadly, you might have made different sense of his words and actions. In this latter case, perhaps he has had an exceptionally good day.)

3. You let your spouse know that you heard him by making eye contact, smiling halfheartedly, giving a backrub, or saying that perhaps supper will cheer him up.

The act of listening can break down at any of these stages. The listener's senses, attention, and brain must be engaged, and the listener must communicate back to the other person that he or she has been heard. Moreover, what I've described is just basic listening. In many cases, emotions and biases also come into play. Sometimes the listener's response to the speaker indicates misunderstanding, and the parties involved must make another attempt to understand each other. And occasionally, the listener's own expectations get in the way of the sense that he or she makes from what the speaker has said. Listening can be complex!

Given the primacy of listening in coaching, wise coaches optimize their chances of listening successfully. Here are some suggestions for doing just that:

■ Practice focusing on one person or activity at a time, no matter how busy you are.

■ Take notes if it helps you absorb what you are hearing. However, don't take notes when the other person is talking about something that is highly significant to him or her. In those instances, eye contact is more important.

■ Change your body language to communicate openness and attentiveness. Turn your shoulders toward the person speaking, adopt an open facial expression—with your facial muscles relaxed and your lips neither pursed nor entirely apart—and keep your eyes on the speaker much of the time, but not constantly because that would make it seem like you are staring.

- Pay attention to the responses you give to communicate that you have heard the speaker and attempted to understand him or her. With people you know well, or in situations that have no risk, such communication is often minimal and needs no prior consideration or even awareness. However, when you are trying to build trust with coaching partners, make your listening responses a bit more explicit.

- Adopt key phrases and terms used by the other speaker. For instance, if you usually call sustained silent reading "SSR time" but a teacher with whom you are working calls it "DEAR (or Drop Everything and Read) time," then when talking to him or her, say, "DEAR time."

Listening is at the heart of all literacy coaching. Start with it and, when in doubt, return to it. Listening for further information is always helpful.

General Tactics for Coaching Communication

What follows are communication tactics that should be in every coach's toolbox. In some ways, they are common sense, and in many situations, they need little thought before using. However, new coaches or coaches in difficult situations may want to pay extra attention to these communication basics.

Silence

One of the most valuable tools that you can have in your tool kit of coaching skills is silence. When a teacher asks a literacy coach a question or tells a literacy coach about a struggle, the coach probably will do what most humans do: attempt to answer. However, I encourage you to wait a moment, about two seconds, before responding. This pause provides two valuable opportunities: First, it gives you the chance to breathe. A deep breath before responding can make you feel centered and calm, and you will be more likely to provide an effective response from that position. Second, the pause gives the other person another chance to say more. You'll be surprised to find that the other person frequently uses this time to provide more information, and in fact, this extra information is often highly valuable.

Think about it: When we prepare to share a problem with someone else, we often think it through logically and prepare an exact statement or step-by-step explanation of what we are struggling with. This prepared information is what comes out in the initial statement or question. When given another second, though, we often tell how we feel or add a less thought-out but still important piece of information. Here are two examples:

Example 1

Teacher: I just don't know what to do with Justin and Marissa. They are both reading much more difficult material than their classmates, and I don't see anything they need from me.

[The literacy coach waits in silence.]

Teacher: I feel so useless!

Example 2

Teacher: What can I do about kids who don't want to revise their writing?

[The literacy coach waits in silence.]

Teacher: I've tried using peer revision, but that doesn't work. I've also tried having conferences with each student, but I can't find the time!

In example 1, the extra moment allows the teacher to share a feeling that reveals self-doubt. That may be the underlying issue for the teacher, and if the literacy coach had jumped in without waiting, the coach might have offered a lot of knowledge-based information about the needs of highly successful readers, when what the teacher really needed was a response to her feelings that she can't help the stronger students. Of course, the statement "I feel so useless" also could just be an off-the-cuff remark. An effective literacy coach would gather more information to determine whether the teacher needed ideas for helping strong readers, bolstering her sense of efficacy, both, or neither.

In example 2, the pause provided by the literacy coach gives the teacher time to tell more about what he has tried in the classroom. The teacher then offers information about what has been tried. This comment gives the literacy coach a great deal more information to build on and from which to learn more.

A moment's silence gives teachers time to elaborate further on what they are thinking or feeling. It also calms the literacy coach and helps him or her focus.

Questioning

Coaches' questions serve two purposes in a coaching conversation: Sometimes they are asked merely to enable coaches to understand a situation, practice, or problem presented by teacher partners, and other times they are asked to prompt further reflection among teachers. The first is for the benefit of the coach, whereas the second is for the benefit of the teacher. Often, questions serve both purposes.

Coaches who are new or unsure of themselves may perceive their role as providing information and advice to teachers. They do this in a low-key, friendly manner, which is how some people perceive coaching. Actually, though, such "telling" is not coaching at all! Coaching is about listening and learning first and telling only occasionally and after ensuring that it is the best option at that moment.

Thus, when teachers approach coaches with problems, questions, or concerns, savvy coaches listen and learn more, using questions as their tool. The range of questions that coaches might use is broad, depending on the situation, but educator/author Parker Palmer (2004) provides a good guideline: Ask questions that are open and honest. Open questions are those for which any answer is acceptable; the asker does not have a preconceived notion of what a "right" answer would be. Honest questions are questions that really are questions; they are not suggestions or opinions disguised as questions. Some examples of the latter are "Have you ever thought of taking a workshop on that?" "Do you think maybe these students are bored?" and "What would you think of asking the assistant principal for help?" If you have a suggestion and feel that it is appropriate to make it, then state it as a suggestion. If you ask a question, make sure that it is one with a variety of acceptable answers and that you want to hear the other person's reply.

Asking a good question sometimes causes a bit of disequilibrium for the receiver, and that prompts a little learning. For instance, if a coach asks, "How does this student construct meaning while reading?" and the teacher has not been focusing on meaning construction, that question might give the teacher pause as he collects his thoughts and shifts, say, from talking about the student's motivation to read to considering the student's construction of meaning. As a result of the coach's question, the teacher begins to reflect on the relationship between motivation and meaning and to notice new things about the student in question.

This example demonstrates how asking a good question can sometimes be the most effective practice that a coach can use. The right question can make one really think, and deeper thinking is almost always conducive to good teaching and learning.

Paraphrasing

When I lead workshops, I visually represent paraphrasing with an image of an ear, which is sometimes surprising to participants who assume that paraphrasing is about what one speaks. Actually, though, good paraphrasing is a reflection of good listening. To paraphrase well, one must listen well enough to be able to repeat what was said with just a little bit of difference. In contrast, repeating what another person said verbatim is mimicking, not paraphrasing.

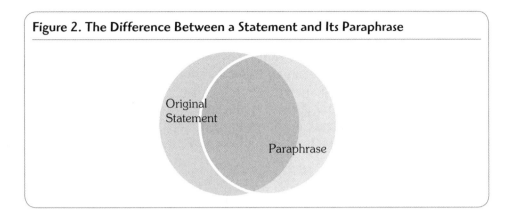

Figure 2. The Difference Between a Statement and Its Paraphrase

Original Statement

Paraphrase

A paraphrase must contain just enough of the listener's own words to demonstrate that what was said was heard and understood.

For instance, if a teacher says, "This science textbook is really hard. I try to give the students a study guide for each chapter, but it seems like only about half the kids can really get through it and understand the important points," it would take only minimal listening skills for the coach to repeat that statement exactly as it was spoken. If the coach really heard the teacher, she might paraphrase by saying, "I hear that you have tried helping your students with this tough science book by giving them study guides, but still only about half the kids are able to understand it." The coach shows that she understood what was said well enough to insert some of her own words.

Figure 2 illustrates the difference between paraphrasing and the original statement. They are almost identical, but there is just enough difference for the speaker to know that the coach heard and understood what was said.

Clarifying

Clarifying is important for ensuring that one has heard accurately. It enhances a coaching relationship by demonstrating the coach's desire to hear well and understand. The act of clarifying demonstrates recognition that even though one has tried to listen and learn, there is still a chance that one has misunderstood.

Coaches often forget to clarify. This may be because they are eager to move ahead in the coaching conversation, often to get to the point where they, the coaches, can provide information or advice. Clarifying slows the conversation down productively and positions coaches as listeners first. Savvy coaches will double-check that they have heard accurately, adding a simple question like, "Did I get that right?" or "Is that correct?"

Summarizing

Summarizing is often done but given little thought. At the end of a conversation or meeting, someone sums up what was discussed or decided, and that's it. There is, however, an art to summarizing, and it is the art of saying just enough but not too much.

Coaches often summarize at the end of a coaching conversation or team meeting. When summarizing, it is not necessary to repeat everything that has been discussed. Summarizing is not paraphrasing. Rather, identify these items in a summary:

- Goals set
- Decisions made
- Next steps

That's it! Keep your summary short and sweet.

Filler Phrases

We humans often use filler phrases in conversation, such as *hmmm* or *uh-huh*, and there is nothing wrong with using them in a coaching conversation. In fact, for most people, it would be really difficult to avoid such filler phrases, because they are habits. However, these little utterances are sometimes misunderstood and therefore cause consternation.

In workshops, I often invite participants to try out filler phrases with different intonations. Volunteers are given a teacher's statement, such as, "I just can't get these students to read!" and then asked to respond with "Hmmm," first with their voice falling as they say it and then with their voice flat and low. To my ears, saying, "Hmmm," with your voice going from high to low sounds judgmental, and saying it with your voice low and flat sounds concerned. Many workshop participants agree, but some hear just the opposite.

The message here is that even short utterances can be misunderstood. Careful coaches will pay attention to how their teacher partners respond during a coaching conversation to ensure that the message the coaches intend to convey is the one being heard.

Well-Chosen Words

The effectiveness of the coaching conversation often lies in the subtleties of language use. When encountering the same situation, one coach says, "Your class was really out of control today!" while another one comments, "Your class felt different from the last time I visited." Each will get a different response from their teacher partners.

When it comes to word choice, effective coaches are precise and objective. They say, "Given that you are disappointed with the results of that assessment…," rather than, "Given that the kids really bombed on that test…," and, "The curriculum represents what we are asked to teach," rather than, "You'll be in trouble if you don't teach the curriculum." When the situation may become tense, wise coaches use bland words rather than spicy ones and speak in simple, declarative statements.

Some terms empower the other person. For instance, questions that begin with *what*, *how*, or *can you tell me* position the other person to say what they mean to say. In contrast, statements that begin with *why*, *why don't you*, *could you*, *isn't*, or *I'd like* leave the speaker in control and put the other person in a one-down position.

Avoid terms that might make the other person feel self-conscious, as though they have said something wrong, even though you likely don't intend to convey that message. *But* is the biggest offender in this regard; it implies that a disagreement will ensue. Other terms that may make your teaching partners feel that they are being contradicted include *actually*, *unfortunately*, and *the truth is*.

Finally, watch your pronouns. Don't say *we* when you mean *you*. For instance, avoid saying, "Why don't we do some more assessment?" if you really mean, "I think you should do some more assessment." The plural *we* is sometimes used to cajole children, and it often feels condescending and manipulative when used with adults. Of course, if you are truly referring to both yourself and your teaching partners, the plural pronoun *we* is entirely appropriate.

"Say Some More About That"

One of my favorite phrases is *say some more about that*. Obviously, these words encourage other people to talk more—to elaborate on their questions, concerns, or observations. This statement demonstrates that a literacy coach is listening, and creates conversational space for the teacher to say more. It also makes explicit that the literacy coach wants or needs some more information.

The effectiveness of *say some more about that* is that it is neutral. It does not commit the speaker to any opinion and does not take the discussion in any particular direction. If, however, a more specific question or statement is made, the discussion may veer in a direction not desired by the teacher. For instance, in the following example, the teacher is struggling with a particular aspect of her spelling program, but the literacy coach's question does not get to the root of the matter:

Teacher:	The kids' writing is so poor. I just don't know what to do.
Literacy coach:	Have you tried using the rubric that the district language arts department has developed?
Teacher:	Yes, but there is so much on the rubric. I can only focus on a little at a time, and I still have so many concerns with the writing I get from the kids.
Literacy coach:	Let's talk about how you introduce the elements of the rubric to your students in your minilessons.

In this example, spelling never even comes up. The literacy coach asks a follow-up question, but it is too directive in shaping the conversation.

For contrast, look at the next example, in which the literacy coach suggests that the teacher "say some more about that."

Teacher:	The kids' writing is so poor. I just don't know what to do.
Literacy coach:	Say some more about that.
Teacher:	Well, we've been writing persuasive essays, and the kids get the idea that they're supposed to give reasons to support their claims.
Literacy coach:	Hmmm.
Teacher:	But the writing I get is so hard to read! I can't tell what the students are trying to say.
Literacy coach:	Say some more, please.
Teacher:	Well, some of the kids are still using invented spelling, and others just, well, they don't think spelling is important.

By asking the teacher to say more, and by using that tactic more than once, the literacy coach learns about the teacher's concerns in greater detail. The ensuing conversation will be much more focused and more likely to attend to what is on the teacher's mind.

Notice that there is sort of a continuum here: You might start with a moment's pause; then, if the person doesn't say more, say "Hmmm"; and finally, ask the person to say more, if more information is still needed. However, don't get too caught up in this sequence. Use it at times, but use any one of the responses whenever you wish as well.

"What Do You Think?"

Annette Sword-Peterson, a literacy coach in Rockford, Illinois, taught me this strategy. She has observed that we often know the answers to our own questions, if we are given enough time and are encouraged to trust ourselves. So, from Annette, I've learned the usefulness of asking, "What do you think?" This question serves several purposes: It demonstrates that the literacy coach values the teacher as a problem solver and decision maker, it shows the literacy coach's belief that there is not just one expert in the room, and it gives the teacher a chance to listen to his or her own inner guide. These benefits can be seen in the following example:

Teacher: Oscar is superb at creating video about what his group has learned, but I don't think he's paying any attention to the content, just the video. Is that OK?

Literacy coach: What do you think?

Teacher: Well, it seems as though he isn't getting everything he should from this project.

[The literacy coach is silent for two seconds.]

Teacher: Although his video talents could be very useful to him in the future, he still needs to produce video *about* something.

Literacy coach: What could you do?

Teacher: Well, maybe I'll talk to him about this in a supportive way so he knows I value his talent. I might use the idea that he'll need research skills if he really wants to make documentaries for a living, as he says he does.

Frequently, we know what we want to do, but we need support in discovering it and doing it. However, there are times when we really are stuck. Because literacy coaches are not mind readers, they cannot be sure which is the case with any given teacher, although there may be clues. After working with a teacher for a while, you may become aware of subtle qualities to the conversation, such as the teacher's tone of voice or facial expression, that indicate whether the teacher is asking for your ideas or needing to explore his or her own. As a literacy coach, you may not be consciously aware of these signals. You may just develop a sense of when the teacher needs help and when the teacher needs support in answering his or her question or solving a problem.

However, you may not have this sense in a particular coaching situation, perhaps because you don't know the teacher well. In such cases, there is little harm in asking, "What do you think?" You can even be explicit and say,

Sometimes I find that I'm most helpful by listening to a teacher's own ideas about how to solve a problem, and other times I'm most helpful when I try to solve the problem. I'm not sure which you need right now. Can you help me?

Remember, there's no need to rush to an answer. Take your time. It will be an investment in the effectiveness of your coaching.

"I Don't Know...Let's Find Out"

As mentioned in previous chapters, one of the greatest dangers for a literacy coach is the temptation to be the expert. Yes, you know some things and have some valuable experience, and you should share your insights freely. However, if you are unsure about something, say so. Let the teacher you are working with know if you don't know.

Saying, "I don't know," can be difficult for many of us, probably because we are human and many people feel like failures if they don't know the answer. If you struggle to admit that you don't know something, you might want to practice admitting it with trusted friends, your spouse or partner, or even your children. Then, you can add this phrase to your literacy coaching tool kit.

The phrase has one benefit in and of itself, at least some of the time, because it demonstrates for the teacher your comfort with not having all the answers. This may make some teachers more comfortable in coming to you when they themselves are lacking information or insight. However, the phrase has additional value not for what it says but for what might happen if you don't use it. Without this phrase, you may muddle through a conversation by trying to fake it, an approach that is likely to be unhelpful to the teacher and may undermine your ability to be effective in the future. Note, however, that the phrase doesn't end with "I don't know." If it did, you might feel ineffective, and the teacher probably would feel frustrated. When you add "Let's find out" to the phrase, you do two things: First, you remind the teacher that he or she is not alone; you, and perhaps others, can work with the teacher to solve the problem or answer the question. Second, by saying, "I don't know...let's find out," you demonstrate what good teaching is all about.

There is a myth in the education profession—and outside it—that a good teacher is one who has no problems. A good teacher goes into the classroom in the morning, teaches effortlessly and effectively all day, and goes home at the end of the day, only to do it all over the next day. Even though we know that every teacher faces problems all day long, too often we feel embarrassed by the teaching problems that we ourselves face. This may be why some teachers prefer to work in isolation and become self-conscious when being observed. It also adds to the fear felt by beginning teachers: They know they are far from having problem-free days, and they can't imagine ever getting to that point.

It's time that we put this myth to rest. The truth is that good teachers are problem solvers. They have a lot of problems and aren't afraid to admit it, probably because they know that one of the ways they can get solutions is by talking about problems with literacy coaches, principals, parents, other teachers, and even students. As a literacy coach, you deliver a powerful message when you demonstrate a problem-solving stance. You also help shift the culture of a school when you take your own ignorance in stride, admit it, and ask a teacher to work with you to figure something out. This approach reminds all educators that problem solving is our business. Here is an example of this communication strategy in action:

Teacher: The kids hate writing in their journals. They've been doing it for years and say they're tired of it. When I tell them it's journal time, they groan. How can I get them to like journaling?

Literacy coach: What do you think?

Teacher: I feel like I've tried everything. Sometimes I give a topic, and other times I let them choose. We've brainstormed topic ideas. I've let them write with buddies. I've let them sit or lie on the rug during journal time. I'm out of ideas! What can I do?

Literacy coach: I'm not sure. Can we work on this together to figure it out?

Teacher: Sure, I could use the help. Where do we begin?

If you as a literacy coach don't know the solution to a problem, admit it. Then, invite the teacher to work with you to solve it. This approach is sincere, helpful, and supportive of collaboration. It conveys that there is no one expert in education and that all educators can be problem solvers.

Conclusion

The communication strategies presented in this chapter—listening well, maintaining silence, enacting a few key tactics, and putting to use a few phrases that encourage teachers to say and reflect more—can be useful to all literacy coaches. I urge you to try these strategies and observe which ones work for you. Also, develop your own tactics that are useful. As you reflect on a particular coaching conversation, presentation, or demonstration, ask yourself about the language you used and why it was or wasn't effective.

I recently heard a colleague present some of her research at a staff meeting. At one point, she recognized that the terms she was using were contradictory, and she declared, "Oh, language is such a problem!" Then, she went on, using the same contradictory terms. I encourage you to do the opposite. Recognize that language sometimes can be a problem, and then become a careful observer of which terms are effective and which aren't. Having a few key phrases in your literacy coaching tool kit can make all the difference.

The communication tools highlighted in this chapter support literacy coaching processes. The most important coaching process, the coaching conversation, is the focus of Chapter 6.

ADDITIONAL RESOURCES

Dimitrius, J.-E., & Mazzarella, M. (1999). *Reading people: How to understand people and predict their behavior—anytime, anyplace.* New York, NY: Ballantine.

Kegan, R., & Lahey, L.L. (2001). *How the way we talk can change the way we work: Seven languages for transformation.* San Francisco, CA: Jossey-Bass.

Nichols, M.P. (1995). *The lost art of listening: How learning to listen can improve relationships.* New York, NY: Guilford.

Tannen, D. (2007). *Talking voices: Repetition, dialogue, and imagery in conversational discourse* (2nd ed.). New York, NY: Cambridge University Press. doi:10.1017/CBO9780511618987

CHAPTER 6

How Do I Facilitate Coaching Conversations?

- Why would I include coaching conversations in my work?
- What is my role during a coaching conversation?
- How can I keep track of coaching conversations?
- What should I do when a teacher repeatedly gets off track during a coaching conversation?
- How do I schedule coaching conversations?

The coaching conversation is the heart of a literacy coach's work. It is valuable for establishing a trusting relationship and understanding your teacher partners. It is where the work begins for coach–teacher collaborations because it provides teachers an opportunity to talk about what is going on for them, in their own classrooms, with their own students. It is the prime opportunity for coaches to perform their first duty, which is listening and learning. This chapter gives coaches the essentials for facilitating effective coaching conversations, recording those conversations, and staying on track.

The Structure of Coaching Conversations

Whether you are having a coaching conversation with an individual or a group of teachers, it is good to have a general sense of where the conversation is going. I created the problem-solving cycle as a guide for coaching conversations and other learning conversations and described it in detail elsewhere (Toll, 2012). Here I summarize this cycle as a model for literacy coaches to use. Refer to Figure 3 for a visual representation of the problem-solving cycle.

The Problem-Solving Cycle

The Problem. To have a problem-solving cycle, you need a problem! Pink (2009) finds that people are motivated to work hard when they are trying to gain more autonomy over their work, achieve greater mastery of their work,

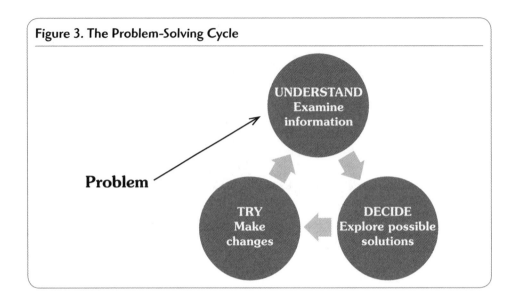

Figure 3. The Problem-Solving Cycle

UNDERSTAND
Examine
information

Problem

TRY
Make
changes

DECIDE
Explore possible
solutions

or work for a greater purpose. For teachers, the latter two seem especially important: Most teachers want to become more effective in what they do, and they often are working for the well-being of their students or the greater good of society. Most teachers want to address obstacles to these goals, and coaching conversations can be great places to do so.

My first step in a coaching conversation, then, is to ask a question that helps the coach identify a problem. I usually ask The Question (Toll, 2006), introduced in Chapter 4, or a variation, as outlined in Table 5.

As your teacher partner answers The Question, continue to probe by asking, "Anything else?" Record every answer you get. It may take 10–15

Table 5. The Question and Variations

The Question	Variations
When you think about the reading and writing that you want your students to do and the teaching that you want to do, what gets in the way?	▪ When you think about the understanding that you want your students to have when they learn [insert content discipline here, such as geography or biology], what gets in the way? ▪ When you think about the way you want to implement [guided reading, vocabulary instruction, etc.] and about the kind of learning that you want your students to do as a result, what gets in the way?

minutes for the teacher to tell you everything that is getting in the way, but be patient. This is valuable information. Record the teacher's responses verbatim. When the teacher cannot think of anything else that is getting in the way, read the list back to the teacher and ask which item he or she would like to focus on in that coaching cycle.

Sometimes your teacher partners will choose a problem that is not the one you would choose for them. Try to go with your partners' selection; in this way, you show that you really do want to start where they are.

Understanding the Problem. Ask questions to better understand the problem and perhaps in the process to help your teacher partner better understand it as well. Try to ask questions about all aspects of the problem. Record your teacher partner's answers to the questions and also any questions that go unanswered. When you have exhausted all possible questions, review the unanswered ones and decide with your partner whether answers to any of them should be found. If so, you and your partner will want to plan to find the answers to those questions.

For instance, let's say that the problem that the teacher identified has to do with some of her students who are not reading accurately. In fact, they frequently guess at words. As you ask questions about these students, you note three questions that your teacher partner was unable to answer: What do these students understand reading to be for? What do the students do when they read silently? and What kind of retellings do the students do? Your teacher partner recognizes that answers to all three of these questions could be helpful to the problem-solving process, so the two of you develop a plan for collecting additional information and then meeting in one week to share what you have learned.

The step in understanding a problem deeply is often overlooked when teachers and coaches discuss a problem. Frequently, the conversation goes from identifying a problem to brainstorming what could be done about it. By pausing to understand the problem better, coaches help teachers use data well, think carefully about what is actually happening, and possibly learn more about the problem. Information from this step will be a big help in the next stage of the cycle. When this step is skipped, teachers often jump into trying something different in a trial-and-error manner, and coaches often make suggestions with little to go on.

Making Decisions. After identifying a problem and taking the time to understand it, the next step in the problem-solving cycle is to set a goal. The question, If this problem were solved, what would it be like? is often helpful in supporting teachers in arriving at a goal that will describe the desired situation. For instance, if the problem being discussed is eighth-grade students' failure to do their homework, when the coach asks the teacher what it would be like if the problem were solved, the teacher might say, "The kids will do their homework every night!" This then becomes the goal.

When a goal is identified, help your teacher partner brainstorm possible steps toward that goal. Encourage thinking broadly, not just about possible instructional strategies but also about alternate classroom arrangements; schedule changes; new formats for students' learning tasks and assignments; creative ways to use the services of special educators, educational assistants, volunteers, and others who work in the classroom; or any of the other aspects that contribute to successful teaching and learning. Again, you and your partners may need to pause to learn some more if you are unable to think of some good next steps. Think together about where to find more ideas (e.g., professional journals, websites, other teachers) and share the task of turning to these resources to find possible steps toward the goal. Then, meet again to add the things you found to the brainstormed list of options. When you have enough possibilities, support your partner as he or she decides what to try.

It is worth spending the time to develop a strong list of options before choosing what to try. If you and your teacher partners rush to decide, then the problem-solving process will not be as helpful; it will lead to quick decisions based on the most obvious information rather than leading to thoughtful reflection and a careful examination of available options.

Trying Something New. When your teacher partners have decided what they want to try, help them plan for implementation and for evaluation of what they have tried. Figure 4 provides a record-keeping sheet that includes space for planning. You can record the steps that your partners plan to take and the approximate timeline for completing them. Of course, teachers implementing something new will find this tool helpful for meeting their goal, but you also will find it helpful in reminding you what your partners are doing and when you might want to check in on them.

The coaching conversation record sheet also provides a chart on which you and your teacher partners can plan for evaluating the actions taken to see if the goal is met. Determine what will be evident if the goal is met—that is, what one will observe, see, or feel—and identify tools to use in collecting that evidence.

Continue the Cycle. After your teacher partners have tried something new and evaluated progress toward the goal, use the additional data from the evaluation to understand the effectiveness of what was tried. Next, decide together whether it is best to continue the new action, tweak it, or discontinue it, and then go from there. A second goal or additional next steps are often identified in this process.

Figure 4. Coaching Conversation Record Sheet

Teacher(s): _____   Grade/subject area: _____

Coach: _____   Date: _____

Topic/problem: _____

Information about the topic/problem: _____

_____

_____

_____

_____

_____

_____

_____

_____

_____

_____

Goal: _____

_____

Brainstormed options for meeting the goal: _____

_____

_____

_____

Action to be taken: _____

_____

_____

_____

_____

_____

(continued)

Figure 4. Coaching Conversation Record Sheet (*Continued*)

Action Plan

Step 1: _____   Date to be done by:

_____   _____

Step 2: _____   Date to be done by:

_____   _____

Step 3: _____   Date to be done by:

_____   _____

Step 4: _____   Date to be done by:

_____   _____

Evaluating success in meeting the goal:

If the Goal Is Met, This Will Be Seen/Heard/Felt:	Tool to Assess Whether This Is Seen/Heard/Felt:

Next meeting date and time: _____

Focus of the next meeting: _____

_____

_____

_____

_____

To do before then: _____

_____

_____

_____

The Literacy Coach's Survival Guide: Essential Questions and Practical Answers (2nd ed.) by Cathy A. Toll.
© 2014 by the International Reading Association.

Record Keeping

It is important to keep track of coaching conversations, to monitor progress, and to remind participants about what has been decided and learned. The Coaching Conversation Record Sheet (Figure 4) is aligned with the problem-solving cycle explained previously. Use the sections of the sheet that apply for each coaching conversation that you have. This sheet is also available on IRA's website (www.reading.org/coachingsheet) as a fillable PDF, which provides adjustable spaces to enter information and can be downloaded for use on your laptop or tablet. You can scan the QR code in the page margin next to the figure to access the form that way, too.

At the end of the chapter, I also provide samples of the record keeping that took place over four sample coaching conversations between Betty Jones (a sixth-grade teacher) and Alison Smith (a literacy coach; both names are pseudonyms) to show how the form might be used to document phases in the coaching conversation.

- *Sample 1:* During the first conversation, Alison helped Betty identify a problem related to three students who seemed to be making random guesses when they read and losing track of meaning in the process. Alison recorded this problem on the record-keeping sheet. She then asked Betty many questions about these boys and their reading and recorded the teacher's answers as information to understand the problem. As they talked, Betty and Alison felt that they needed more information about the students being discussed, so they planned to learn more by gathering additional data about the students' understanding of reading and their meaning construction when they read. Betty agreed to interview each boy using the Burke Reading Interview (Goodman, Watson, & Burke, 2005) to determine whether the boys understood that reading is about meaning construction; she also decided to ask them to do retellings of informational text that they had read silently, to evaluate their meaning construction with silent reading, because up until then she had only been paying attention to the boys' oral reading. Meanwhile, Alison agreed to meet with the boys in a small group and engage them in a Directed Reading–Thinking Activity (DRTA; Rasinski & Padak, 2004), another method for observing students' meaning construction when reading silently. Betty and Alison agreed to meet the following week to share what they had learned. At the bottom of the record-keeping sheet, Alison recorded the date and time of the next meeting, its purpose, and the tasks that they each would do before then.

- *Sample 2:* In their second coaching conversation, Betty and Alison shared what they learned from their further investigations, which led to the insight that one of the three students being discussed was reading more effectively than originally thought. This student's retelling as well as his answers to questions on the Burke Reading Interview and his predictions on the DRTA demonstrated fairly good attention to the meaning of what he read. Betty still had some concerns about him, though, because when he read aloud, he didn't seem to use fix-up strategies when the meaning fell apart, so she and Alison made a note to pursue a second goal about teaching all three boys fix-up strategies, which they would attend to after the first goal was met. The evidence collected about the other two boys indicated that they were not attending to meaning when they read silently and that they did not articulate anything about meaning construction when they discussed reading in the Burke Reading Interview. Alison recorded all of this information in the "Information about the topic/problem" section of the record sheet, in place of the information that was recorded there from the first coaching conversation. A goal for the first two boys was identified, which was that they would attend to the meaning of what they read, and options for meeting this goal were brainstormed. Alison recorded the goal as well as the brainstormed options. Betty thought several of the brainstormed options could help the boys and didn't want to select only one, so she decided on a plan of action that would incorporate three of the choices into a series of guided reading lessons: She would demonstrate her own meaning construction through think-alouds and help the boys start doing the same; she would read aloud with intentional miscues and ask the boys to signal when the meaning was disrupted; and then she would have the boys read aloud, being prepared for her to ask, "Did that make sense?" at any point. Alison recorded this action plan as well as the steps to be taken in implementing it. Then, she and Betty identified two pieces of evidence that could be collected at the end of the plan to determine if the goal was met: the students' retellings of material to determine if the boys were constructing meaning and the students' responses to a second administration of the Burke Reading Interview to determine if the boys understood that reading was about meaning. Betty and Alison agreed to meet at the midpoint of the implementation of the action plan to see how it was going.

- *Sample 3:* At their third meeting a few weeks later, Betty and Alison discussed how the guided reading groups were going, and Alison recorded that information in the "Information about the topic/problem" section of the record-keeping sheet. The groups were going well, so the conversation was shorter than the others and ended with Alison recording the date and time of their next meeting, when they would discuss the evaluation of the goal.

- *Sample 4:* Betty and Alison's fourth meeting consisted primarily of a discussion of the two assessments that Betty did to determine whether the goal was met. Both the Burke Reading Interview and the retelling activity led Betty to conclude that the boys were indeed constructing meaning as they read. Thus, Betty and Alison decided that it was time to begin work on the next goal, which would address the problem that these two boys as well as the third one included in their earlier conversation did not seem to use fix-up strategies when meaning fell apart in their reading. Betty and Alison set a time to meet to begin that next coaching cycle and ended their meeting with a high five in celebration of Betty's success in the first cycle.

In this four-step example, Alison recorded each conversation on a new record-keeping sheet but copied and pasted some pieces from one sheet to the next. In this way, she preserved the goal, action plan, and evaluation plan developed in the second session for the third and fourth conversations. However, she changed some information every time the pair met. There is no hard-and-fast rule about this. I encourage coaches to make the notes from each session as helpful as possible in remembering what was discussed, what decisions were made, and what next steps will be taken.

Some coaches find the space on such a record-keeping sheet too constrictive and decide to record the same items but in a notebook or Word document that is open-ended, without particular spaces or items on the sheet. Such an approach can work well, too. The important thing is to take good notes and find a system that works for you.

Be sure to give a copy of your record-keeping sheet to your teacher partners as soon as possible after each coaching session. If you record your notes digitally, you can send them to your partners almost immediately as an e-mail attachment.

Avoid giving notes of coaching conversations to principals or other supervisors. These notes should be a place to record in detail the struggles, actions, and successes of your teacher partners. As such, they are not materials for supervisors but rather should feel like safe spaces to record teachers' collaborations with you. (Note: In the first edition of this book, I suggested that giving notes to principals was an option. Over the last decade, it has become clear to me that that is not a good idea.)

When There Is No Problem

Coaching conversations often address problems that teachers encounter in their work. As I discussed previously, Pink's (2009) work demonstrates that most people want to work hard to overcome obstacles to doing better or accomplishing a purpose. Occasionally, though, teachers choose to pursue a topic of interest in a coaching conversation, not to solve a problem but to enhance what they are already doing. For instance, some first-grade teachers may want to use the coaching partnership to incorporate the arts into reading and math instruction, while a middle school science teacher may wish to collaborate with a coach in using digital tablets to help students write lab reports.

In these instances, the coaching conversation has the same structure as the problem-solving cycle. Beyond identifying an interest or enhancement rather than a problem, the partners spend time understanding the topic, setting a goal, finding a way to reach the goal, and trying it out through an action plan and a plan for evaluation. Coaches will be just as effective following the process described previously and using the coaching strategies found throughout this book when helping teachers expand on their successes as they are when they help teachers solve problems impeding their success.

Why, then, do I start with a question about what gets in the way of success? I do this because our struggles are usually our strongest motivators. Think about your personal life: You went on that diet because you couldn't get into last winter's pants, and you cleaned the basement because you couldn't find the holiday wreath, right? Indeed, there are occasions when we are motivated by a wish rather than a challenge, and those occasions will rise to the forefront when teachers and coaches collaborate, but starting with The Question is usually the most productive start to a coaching cycle.

Scheduling Coaching Conversations

I encourage literacy coaches to schedule coaching conversations on a regular basis. A question to consider is, How often do I need to meet with my teacher partners in order to keep the work flowing but not overwhelm them? When coaching conversations are scheduled too far apart from each other, they feel disjointed, if they feel like conversations at all. However, when coaching conversations occur too frequently, they fail to provide adequate time between meetings for assessments and other tasks that have been agreed upon.

Aim to schedule coaching conversations *every* one or two weeks if at all possible. If you can establish a regular time, such as the first and third Monday of every month at 3:30 p.m., then teachers can put you into their schedules for the entire year, and everyone can count on that time being available. If you find it impossible to schedule very many coaching conversations, reflect on whether there is a bigger problem, such as too large a workload for teacher partners, too little of your time available for coaching conversations, or too many teachers unwilling to engage in coaching collaborations. Talk to your own supervisor—not about teachers but about your own work—if one of these seems to be the case.

Whenever possible, have coaching conversations in teachers' classrooms. By meeting in classrooms, you convey that you are there for the teachers, not the other way around. In addition, your teacher partners will have on hand instructional materials and samples of the students' work that might be relevant for the conversation.

If you are a literacy coach in a large school and can't regularly get to all the teachers for individual coaching conversations, then you might divide the staff into quarters. You could focus on having regular coaching conversations with, say, teachers in the science department during the first quarter, teachers in social studies during the second quarter, and so on. It is not an ideal situation—the ideal is to have regular coaching conversations with each teacher all year long—but it is a tolerable compromise for an overextended literacy coach.

An even better solution, but one that requires the school's leadership to understand coaching well, is to ask the school improvement team (or whatever team it is that includes administrators and teachers and sets direction for the entire school) to identify a *pool* of teachers that you will work with. That pool is created by examining schoolwide staffing, student placement, and data and determining where teaching is especially challenging. For instance, in an elementary school where primary classrooms have a much lower ratio of adults to students because of smaller class sizes and additional teaching assistants, teaching may be especially challenging in grades 4 and 5. Or in a middle school where English learners are placed in one house at each grade level, teaching may be especially challenging in those houses. At the high school level, a team may determine that teaching is especially challenging in the text-heavy social studies and science courses. Note that in all of these cases, the phrase *especially challenging* is used to convey that teaching in these situations has additional challenges, not to suggest that teachers not in these situations are not challenged. Also, note that the pool is identified without reference to the quality of teaching that is taking place; a coach would be very lonely if a school leadership team suggested that the pool of teachers working with the coach was made up of the school's least effective teachers, because no one would want to be in that group!

When scheduling coaching conversations, work as best as you can with the teachers' schedules to find the most convenient and least disruptive times. Schedule individual conversations for 30 minutes and small-group conversations for 45–60 minutes. If teachers are guaranteed a duty-free lunch period, do your best not to use that time for literacy coaching conversations. Resist the urge to meet for shorter periods of time, because all involved will likely feel hurried or unproductive. I find that if I'm rushed, I'm much less effective as a literacy coach. I tend to do less listening and jump to the planning stage sooner than I would otherwise.

Coaches' Tasks During Coaching Conversations

In addition to the communication strategies outlined in Chapter 5, there are tasks that coaches perform routinely to ensure the effectiveness of the coaching conversation: getting started, checking in, steering, and planning.

Getting Started

Be fairly direct in starting coaching conversations. You don't want small talk to take up too much of the precious time available. When meeting with teacher partners for the first time, start out by saying something like, "Thanks for meeting with me. As you know, I am meeting with each of the teachers [or teams] to listen and learn and find out how we can partner together to solve problems or pursue topics of interest."

When meeting with teacher partners for the second or subsequent time, start by thanking participants for meeting with you and briefly reviewing what was discussed at the last meeting. Use your record-keeping notes as a guide. Here's what this part of the conversation might sound like:

> Thanks for meeting with me. I have my notes from our last conference here. Let's see, we discussed your literacy centers and your sense that they aren't going well. After discussing them at length, you identified a specific area that you would like to work on, which is assessing the effectiveness of your center time. The goal you set was that you would develop a plan for ongoing assessment of the activities in your centers and the students' use of center time. We agreed to meet today to think about how you might meet that goal and develop a plan.

Starting coaching conversations in this manner accomplishes several things. First, literacy coaches provide their teacher partners with a helpful review of what was discussed in the last coaching conversation or provide a sense of what will happen in an initial conversation. Second, literacy coaches focus attention on the work at hand. Without such a focus, coaching conversations often meander, resulting in chitchat, complaining, or rambling without purpose.

Checking In

Coaches sometimes want to check in with their teacher partners before getting into the work that was planned. Thus, after getting started in the manner just described, some coaches then say, "But before we jump in, let me ask, how is it going?" This question shifts the conversation to teacher partners and allows them to talk about whatever is on their minds. The advantage is that it creates an opportunity for teachers to bring up new issues or just give their coach partner an idea of how they are feeling at that time. The risk is that the conversation could veer from what had been planned for that session. If you decide to ask this question, then have a repertoire of strategies to use when teachers raise new problems or new areas of interest that they would like to pursue. Savvy coaches might say something like, "That sounds like another topic that you would like us to address. Shall I put it on the list of things getting in the way, from our first meeting, so we don't lose track of it when we start another cycle of coaching?"

Of course, if a teacher raises an issue that really does seem to be urgent, you may want to invite the teacher to make it the topic of conversation and put the original plan on the back burner. Be cautious, though, about doing this too often, because it puts you and your coaching partner at risk of never resolving a problem or fully exploring a topic of interest. In fact, coaches occasionally encounter teacher partners who repeatedly change the subject; in these situations, wise coaches draw on another question in their repertoire: What do you think is getting in the way for us as we try to come back to the same topic each week?

Steering

I have used ballroom dancing as a metaphor for coaching in part to suggest the degree of direction that a coach provides. In a coaching conversation, the coach is indeed the "lead dancer" and does indeed need to steer. However, just as the lead in a dance uses only a little pressure on his partner's shoulder or back, so a coach provides only the subtlest direction.

Conversations between coaches and teachers, like all human conversations, can get off track. The light touch of a coach permits occasional digressions but ensures that the overall arc of the conversation is productive and related to the topic at hand. Much of this task relies on a coach's human relations skills, and as such there is no prescription for success. However, here are a few tips that may help:

- After sharing a good story or a good laugh, quietly sigh and say, "OK, back to work!"
- If a digression points out a new problem or topic for pursuit in a coaching conversation, offer to make note of it so the team remembers it when starting the next coaching cycle.
- If you truly enjoy the stories or jokes the other person tells, suggest that you get together for lunch so as not to use up time set aside for the coaching conversation.

- Ask for help: "I can tell that if we aren't careful, we'll never get back to the topic at hand! Can you help me out in staying on task?"
- When in doubt about whether to speak up or let a digression continue, give yourself another minute to listen and reflect. If the value of the conversation is unclear, you likely need to hear a bit more of it.
- Think of these moments like you think of *teachable moments* in your classroom. Typically, teachers ask themselves about the value of digressions when deciding whether to continue or go back to the subject at hand. Similarly, you can reflect, albeit quickly, on whether a digression is valuable to the coaching conversation—for instance, because it helps participants connect to one another or because the topic needs to be discussed before participants are ready to move on.

Planning

Coaching conversations should serve as springboards to action. Use the problem-solving cycle and good coaching strategies to help teacher colleagues learn more about problems or how to address them, develop plans for pursuing goals, and evaluate the effectiveness of what is tried. In trying to meet the demands of everyday life in school, some educators are too quick to take action without talking about and understanding the problems that they are addressing. Conversely, some educators want to do nothing *but* talk! As the facilitator of the coaching conversation, you are not in charge of the people who are participating, but you *are* in charge of the process. Ensure that coaching conversations lead to change in classrooms; otherwise, it will be difficult to establish the value of your work as a coach.

In addition, always plan for your next meeting before a coaching conversation ends. Determine the date, time, and location of the meeting and record any steps that will be taken by participants before then. In addition, touch briefly on the focus of the next conversation.

Conclusion

Coaching conversations are an important part of literacy coaches' duties. These conversations enable literacy coaches and teachers to focus on needs, strengths, and concerns that are unique to the participants or of highest priority to them. Successful coaching conversations depend on literacy coaches' facilitation. Among the facilitation skills that are useful for coaching conversations are the following:

- Preparing for the coaching conversation by reviewing previous notes and thinking ahead to what may be discussed in the upcoming coaching conversation
- Taking careful notes to track information about problems or topics of interest, goals, action steps, plans for evaluating the goal, and details of the next meeting
- Keeping the conversation comfortable but focused
- Following through on commitments in a reliable manner

Everything in this chapter works well in coaching partnerships with individuals or with small groups. However, additional suggestions for working with teams are addressed in Chapter 7.

ADDITIONAL RESOURCES

Costa, A.L., & Garmston, R.J. (2002). *Cognitive coaching: A foundation for Renaissance schools* (2nd ed.). Norwood, MA: Christopher-Gordon.

Danielson, C. (2009). *Talk about teaching! Leading professional conversations.* Reston, VA: National Association of Secondary School Principals; Thousand Oaks, CA: Corwin.

Fournies, F.F. (2000). *Coaching for improved work performance* (Rev. ed.). New York, NY: McGraw-Hill.

Toll, C.A. (2012). *Learnership: Invest in teachers, focus on learning, and put test scores in perspective.* Thousand Oaks, CA: Corwin.

Sample Coaching Conversation Record Sheet 1

Teacher(s): Betty Jones _____ Grade/Subject area: Grade 6

Coach: ___ Alison Smith _____ Date: _____ October 17 _____

Topic/problem: Some of Betty's students guess unproductively as they read.

Information about the topic/problem: _____

- Three boys do this.
- The first letters of the boys' guesses have graphophonic similarity to what is on the page.
- Betty has tried having them read with more successful readers, use bookmarks, and tell her whether what they read is making sense.
- In reply to Betty's questions, these boys often say that what they just read does not make sense; they seem to recognize that there is no meaning, but they plow ahead nonetheless.

Goal: _____

Brainstormed options for meeting the goal: _____

Action to be taken: _____

(continued)

Sample Coaching Conversation Record Sheet 1 (*Continued*)

Action Plan

Step 1: _____   Date to be done by:

_____   _____

Step 2: _____   Date to be done by:

_____   _____

Step 3: _____   Date to be done by:

_____   _____

Step 4: _____   Date to be done by:

_____   _____

Evaluating success in meeting the goal:

If the Goal Is Met, This Will Be Seen/Heard/Felt:	Tool to Assess Whether This Is Seen/Heard/Felt:

Next meeting date and time: _October 27, 2:00_____

Focus of the next meeting: _____

_Findings from gathering additional information about these readers_____

_____

_____

_____

To do before then: _____

Betty: Burke Interview with each student; Betty: 1:1 conferences w/ retellings;

Alison: guided reading groups focused on Directed Reading-Thinking Activity

_____

_____

Sample Coaching Conversation Record Sheet 2

Teacher(s): ___Betty Jones___   Grade/Subject area: ___Grade 6___

Coach: ___Alison Smith___   Date: ___October 24___

Topic/problem: ___Some of Betty's students guess unproductively as they read.___

Information about the topic/problem: _____

- Steve: Told main points in retelling; indicates that reading is about "getting the story"; makes logical predictions in DRTA activity

- Lucas: Little meaning construction in retelling and no predictions in DRTA; reading is about "going smooth and pretty fast."

- Vic: Retold only characters' names and name of dog; DRTA predictions were not logical; reading is about "knowing the words."

Goal: ___Lucas and Vic will attend to the meaning of what they read.___

Brainstormed options for meeting the goal: ___Tell them what reading is for; think aloud for Betty to demonstrate meaning construction; have boys pursue answers to a question of interest via information texts; more DRTA; author study—focus on author's intention/thinking/craft; read aloud and ask boys to signal when meaning falls apart (after Betty makes intentional miscues); ask boys as they read, Did that make sense?___

Action to be taken: ___Form a guided reading group with Vic and Lucas with these activities over a series of sessions: Betty does think-alouds as she reads, then supports boys in doing same; Betty also makes intentional miscues as she reads aloud and has the boys hold up stop signs as they catch them; then boys read aloud, and Betty stops frequently to ask, Did that make sense? (whether meaning was disrupted or not)___

(continued)

Sample Coaching Conversation Record Sheet 2 (*Continued*)

Action Plan

Step 1: _Schedule guided reading group into lesson plans._   Date to be done by:
           October 26

Step 2: _Select materials and plan guided reading lessons._   Date to be done by:
           November 3

Step 3: _Meet with boys 3X/week for 2 weeks._   Date to be done by:
           November 17

Step 4: _Evaluate efforts to see if goal is met._   Date to be done by:
           November 20

Evaluating success in meeting the goal:

If the Goal Is Met, This Will Be Seen/Heard/Felt:	Tool to Assess Whether This Is Seen/Heard/Felt:
Students construct meaning as they read.	Retelling
Students understand that reading is about meaning.	Burke Reading Interview

Next meeting date and time: _November 8, 2:00_

Focus of the next meeting: _Check in to see how the guided reading group is going._

To do before then: _Betty: Plan for and begin implementing guided reading group._

Sample Coaching Conversation Record Sheet 3

Teacher(s): __Betty Jones__   Grade/Subject area: __Grade 6__

Coach: __Alison Smith__   Date: __November 8__

Topic/problem: __Some of Betty's students guess unproductively as they read.__

Information about the topic/problem: _____

    Betty has met with Lucas and Nic three times for guided reading lessons on meaning construction. She reports that they are going well. The boys are catching her intentional miscues when she reads aloud and have made some progress in doing their own retellings. She is ready to have them read aloud in next week's sessions, during which she will stop them intermittently and ask if what they are reading makes sense, whether they have miscued or not, to get them in the habit of monitoring their meaning construction as they read. After that, she will evaluate the boys' progress.

Goal: __Lucas and Vic will attend to the meaning of what they read.__

Brainstormed options for meeting the goal: _____

Action to be taken: __Keep up the good work!__

(continued)

Sample Coaching Conversation Record Sheet 3 (*Continued*)

Action Plan

Step 1: _Schedule guided reading group into lesson plans._   Date to be done by:
_____   _October 26_

Step 2: _Select materials and plan guided reading lessons._   Date to be done by:
_____   _November 3_

Step 3: _Meet with boys 3X/week for 2 weeks._   Date to be done by:
_____   _November 17_

Step 4: _Evaluate efforts to see if goal is met._   Date to be done by:
_____   _November 20_

Evaluating success in meeting the goal:

If the Goal Is Met, This Will Be Seen/Heard/Felt:	Tool to Assess Whether This Is Seen/Heard/Felt:
Students construct meaning as they read.	Retelling
Students understand that reading is about meaning.	Burke Reading Interview

Next meeting date and time: _November 22, 2:00_

Focus of the next meeting: _Evaluate progress toward goal._

_____

_____

To do before then: _Betty: Continue with guided reading group._

_____

_____

Sample Coaching Conversation Record Sheet 4

Teacher(s): ___Betty Jones___ Grade/Subject area: ___Grade 6___

Coach: ___Alison Smith___ Date: ___November 22, 2:00___

Topic/problem: ___Some of Betty's students guess unproductively as they read.___

Information about the topic/problem: _____

___Betty readministered the Burke Reading Interview; both boys referred to___

___constructing meaning as a strategy, and both said they thought their teacher would___

___help struggling students think about whether what they read made sense. Betty___

___also asked each boy to do a retelling of a book chapter that they had just read;___

___both boys provided the main idea, Vic provided several supporting ideas, and Lucas___

___provided one supporting idea.___

Goal: ___Lucas and Vic will attend to the meaning of what they read.___

Brainstormed options for meeting the goal: _____

Action to be taken: _____

___Move on to second goal of providing fix-up strategies to Steve, Lucas, and Vic.___

(continued)

Sample Coaching Conversation Record Sheet 4 (*Continued*)

Action Plan

Step 1: Schedule guided reading group into lesson plans. Date to be done by:
October 26

Step 2: Select materials and plan guided reading lessons. Date to be done by:
November 3

Step 3: Meet with boys 3X/week for 2 weeks. Date to be done by:
November 17

Step 4: Evaluate efforts to see if goal is met. Date to be done by:
November 20

Evaluating success in meeting the goal:

If the Goal Is Met, This Will Be Seen/Heard/Felt:	Tool to Assess Whether This Is Seen/Heard/Felt:
Students construct meaning as they read.	Retelling
Students understand that reading is about meaning.	Burke Reading Interview

Next meeting date and time: December 4, 2:00

Focus of the next meeting: _____

Brainstorm how to meet next goal, select an option, and plan for implementation.

To do before then: Celebrate success.

CHAPTER 7

What Is Unique About
Working With Teams?

- Why should I coach teacher teams?
- What should I do when one person dominates a team or group?
- What should I do about people who speak too much or too little?
- What should I do when team or group members disagree or debate?
- How can I help teams improve their functioning?

When I wrote the first edition of this book, literacy coaches worked much more often with individuals than with teams. In fact, I included a small section explaining why it might be valuable for coaches to collaborate with teams, because I thought coaches needed convincing. Now we know that collaborating on teams is an excellent way for teachers to enhance their students' learning. The question then is not whether coaches should work with teams but, rather, how coaches can be most effective in their work with teams.

In some ways, coaching conversations with teams are the same as coaching conversations with individuals; there's just more to say because there are more teachers involved. On the other hand, effective coaches have a few unique strategies and perspectives for working with teams. This chapter will help literacy coaches think about their role with teams and about ways to enhance coaching conversations with teams. In addition, I give a few tips for avoiding common pitfalls of teamwork and provide a tool for understanding how teams evolve over time.

A Word About Terms

In some schools, gatherings of teachers for collaboration are called professional learning communities (PLCs), and in others they are called professional learning teams (PLTs).

The use of the term *learning communities* reflects the thinking of leaders in the corporate world as well as in education that there are entire organizations that might be called learning communities because there is a commitment to continual learning among all members of the workplace. Thus, some leaders think of the entire school as a learning community. For instance, Rick Dufour, a well-known authority in this area, generally conceptualizes the learning community as the entire school, meaning that there is a schoolwide commitment to focusing on student learning and collaborating to increase that learning through teachers' own professional learning (Dufour & Eaker, 1998). When this work occurred in small groups within these schools, participants started referring to those small groups as professional learning communities as well.

Some of us, myself included, would rather not confuse matters by using a term, *professional learning community*, that is used sometimes in reference to an entire school and sometimes to refer to a small group within a school. Therefore, we choose *professional learning team*.

At this point, both terms are used acceptably to describe small groups of teachers, so please don't worry if you are used to *communities* and you notice that I use *teams* or *PLTs* in this book.

Coaches' Roles With PLTs

The obvious role for coaches when working with teams is that of facilitator. After all, the most successful coaches have a high level of skill in processes that help others collaborate. These coaches are process experts. Therefore, many teachers recognize that coaches make great facilitators for the collaborative work in which PLTs engage. When coaches facilitate, they help participants set an agenda and stick to it, ensure that notes are taken, and remind everyone to decide on the next meeting time, location, and topic before adjourning. And when the PLT wishes to engage in a problem-solving cycle, coaches are perfectly positioned as facilitators to steer the process.

Sometimes teachers meet in teams not only for professional learning to enhance student learning, which is the aim of PLTs, but also to attend to administrative tasks, to share information, and to plan initiatives or events. In some schools, there is a pattern of alternating between one kind of activity and another on a regular schedule; in many other schools, PLTs are left to their own devices to decide what to do at any given meeting; and in still other schools, there is so much work assigned to PLTs that these teams never get around to professional learning. In my ideal world, teachers would always be learning together collaboratively, but alas that isn't always the case in reality.

For this reason, coaches might not always assume the facilitator role. They are likely excellent choices to facilitate when PLTs have other tasks that do not involve professional learning, but that is not the best use of coaches' time. Rather, it may be just as productive for another member of the PLT to facilitate and for the coach to be involved only when the team is truly engaged in learning collaboratively. When not facilitating, coaches then choose to be participants or not. Participating in meetings even when they do not involve professional learning allows coaches a chance to learn about other matters that are relevant to their teacher partners and to show their support for the other work that is taking place. However, most coaches find that there are too many teams for them to participate in all of them when the teams are not engaged in professional learning.

A third option for coaches, beyond facilitating and merely participating in team meetings, is to show their support of teams without actually attending all of their meetings. This might be done by providing resources to teams, by offering training or problem solving for team facilitators, or by connecting team initiatives to coaching efforts. An example of the latter would be a coach who learns that teams in the school are working on curriculum alignment, so the coach varies The Question for a bit by asking, "When you think about the effects of curriculum alignment on your teaching, and when you think about how an aligned curriculum could enhance student learning, what is getting in the way?"

Table 6 provides an overview of the roles that coaches might have when working with PLTs. Please note that in the rest of this chapter, I am referring to coaches' work when they are in the facilitator role.

Enhancing the Coaching Conversation With Teams

The communication strategies from Chapter 5 and the strategies for facilitating the coaching conversation in Chapter 6 serve coaches well when they work with PLTs. To make the coaching conversation even more successful, focus on these matters as well.

Choosing a Topic

Choosing a topic takes longer with teams. As you ask The Question, you will hear many more responses. Be patient and keep checking with participants to see if they have any additional items that are getting in the way of their success and their students' success. It may be helpful to use a whiteboard or piece of chart paper to record replies so everyone around the table can see what has been said. When there are no more responses to The Question, ask team members to each identify their top priority for the problem-solving cycle. Mark on the list the choice that each participant makes. If there are five teachers on the team, you will have no more than five items marked, and maybe fewer if some participants choose the same item. Then, ask the team to select the topic from those items that have been marked.

Table 6. Coaches' Roles With Teams

Role	Goal	Key Tasks	Pros	Cons
Facilitator	Lead processes that support collaborative learning	▪ Lead agenda setting ▪ Facilitate problem solving the cycle ▪ Draw attention to data, the content of instruction, and pedagogy ▪ Ensure note-taking ▪ Lead planning for the next meeting	▪ Greatest level of influence on team work ▪ Takes advantage of coaches' process skills	▪ Requires a great deal of coaches' time
Participant	Learn alongside colleagues	▪ Contribute to discussion ▪ Subtly suggest processes to smooth team functions	▪ Provides leadership roles for others (facilitators) ▪ More manageable regarding the time required ▪ Can be alternated with facilitation of teams ▪ Enables coaches to remain aware of teachers' learning	▪ Teams fail to benefit fully from coaches' process skills. ▪ Teachers may feel confused about coaches' shift from coaching one-to-one to participating on teams.
Supporter	Augment team success by providing tools and tactics	▪ Provide resources ▪ Share tools and tactics with team facilitators ▪ Connect to coaching	▪ Keeps the coach engaged ▪ Gives modest support to teacher team learning ▪ Strengthens teachers' facilitation skills	▪ Coaches may be too distant from teams to know how to help.

Earlier in my own work, I attempted to facilitate the group's process of choosing the priority topic from among those identified by participants. I even described that process in an earlier book. However, I have learned that this process, although democratic, takes so long that it just isn't worth it. Team members feel frustrated because they spend so much time in selecting a topic, and they resent me for asking it of them. Therefore, instead, I now just help the team reduce the list to those items selected as a priority by each participant and then sit back while the group makes a decision about their top priority. At worst, someone doesn't get his or her way, but surely everyone will survive, and the advantage is that the group can move on fairly quickly.

Brainstorming

When brainstorming how to meet a goal, remember that there are a lot of ideas in the group. To optimize the chance that group members will comfortably share what they are thinking, remind them that at this point in the process, ideas are merely being brainstormed, without any evaluation. Provide plenty of wait time as well. If you are concerned about the comfort that team members will have in sharing ideas, or if you expect that it will take too long to engage in brainstorming, consider having participants quickly record their brainstormed ideas on sticky notes, one idea per note, without discussing them, and then place the sticky notes on a poster board or whiteboard. Invite participants to follow up by doing a silent sort, in which they rearrange the sticky notes on the board, clustering similar items and grouping related items, all without talking. After a few minutes, you will have a pretty good display of possibilities for meeting the desired goal.

When it comes time to choose among the brainstormed ideas, it may not be necessary for participants to select only one. Sometimes group members each decide to try a different approach to meeting the goal, and then to share results. Other times, group members identify a cluster of similar ideas, and then each participant tries something that is slightly different but in the same vein. These approaches take advantage of the number of teachers in the PLT to recognize that several approaches could be tried simultaneously.

Evaluating

Just as the number of participants allows for more ideas and more actions, it also provides more people to evaluate progress toward a goal. Help group members divide evaluation tasks if they are all trying the same thing; for instance, if a group of four decides to try a new vocabulary strategy, each teacher may use a different tool for evaluating whether students are learning new vocabulary. On the other hand, if each PLT member is trying something different, you may want to use the same evaluation tool for all; otherwise, discrepancies in evaluation results could reflect that the activities were evaluated differently.

Additional Facilitation Tips

In Western society, we tend to think that people automatically know how to communicate in groups and that understanding will automatically occur if communication takes place. Some researchers have attempted to identify the rules for getting people to communicate successfully in groups, but others find that communication is never going to be entirely successful. This makes collaboration in groups challenging! Here are some tips for coaches to help them help PLTs.

Clarify Roles. Earlier in this chapter, I suggested roles that coaches might take when PLTs meet. Savvy coaches discuss their role with a PLT rather than assuming that they know what will be best for the group. This inquiry might have two components: First, ask participants what they hope will happen during their PLT. If they have had coaching conversations with you previously, whether individually or in a group, ask if they hope to do the same in the present group; if they are not familiar with coaching conversations, help them understand this option. Then, if coaching conversations are part of the work that the PLT will engage in, collaborate with participants in deciding how often you should facilitate those conversations and whether the group wants some meetings in which they address other matters.

Honor Varying Levels of Participation. Group leaders often are outgoing people and, therefore, tend to assume that everyone else in the group should be that way, too. Of course, some people are quite shy, and for them active group participation may mean sitting quietly while their minds race with the ideas that they are hearing. The good thing about facilitating a group of adults is that most participants know how they best participate in a group. Therefore, I encourage literacy coaches to ask group members to talk about their participation preferences when the group first meets and then check in with the group members periodically outside the group meetings to see if they are comfortable with their level of participation.

Facilitate Disagreement. Despite the reality that all people experience disagreement from time to time, we sometimes become uncomfortable or even embarrassed when disagreement occurs in a PLT. Literacy coaches can help with this challenge. First, demonstrate your own comfort when disagreement occurs. Show acceptance and curiosity when others disagree with you, and disagree with others in a manner that is without judgment—merely a disagreement, not anything to cause shame, and always done respectfully.

The goal is to have a voice in the conversation but not in a way that leaves others feeling like they can't do the same. Flaherty (1999) suggests that the coach's goal is "mutual freedom of expression" (p. 56) among all participants.

In addition, ask group members what they want to do about disagreements. They'll probably look at you in amazement because this kind of conversation usually doesn't take place in groups, and they'll probably quickly assure you that disagreement is fine. When a disagreement does occur, however, you may want to ask again. Then, group members may better understand why you asked that question.

Address Competing Claims. One source of disagreement in PLTs is competing claims. For example, a group member says that a teaching practice will work well with students, and another group member states, "Not with my students." Or one member of the group makes a claim about what works, and another says, "The research says the opposite." How does a literacy coach help in such situations?

Again, model calm acceptance of disagreement. You might even chuckle and observe, "This happens a lot in education, doesn't it? We face competing claims and have to decide how to resolve them—or if they can be resolved at all." In this manner, you are making disagreement visible and acceptable.

A general approach to competing claims is to offer the suggestion that group members seek an "and"; in other words, encourage participants to seek the best information from both parties in the dispute. This isn't a suggestion that people agree to disagree but, rather, an encouragement to think about why, say, a piece of research might produce one finding and a teacher's classroom might produce another and, if possible, that participants learn what they can from both sources.

If members of a group make competing claims about "the research," you could ask them to share that research. Those who are merely posturing will usually "forget" or become too busy to locate the research they've mentioned. Those who are serious will share the research, which can lead to a valuable discussion about how educators can make decisions when research studies produce competing results. A word of caution: If you ask someone to produce supporting research, do so in a neutral manner. Don't say, "Can you prove it by showing us the research?" or something similar that sounds like a challenge. Rather, say something such as,

> I hear that we have competing claims being made about the research. If you'd give me some citations, I'll track down the research you're referring to. I'll also see if there is anything in the professional literature that would help us understand these competing claims.

If group members make competing claims about their students and what works in their own classrooms, you may want to suggest the following criteria for determining an effective practice:

- It improves students' work and attitudes.
- It is consistent with what you believe about learning, literacy, and teaching.
- It fits the parameters in which you must work, including standards and curricula.

At this point, you may be wondering if my suggestions are a bit naive. After all, people in groups often make competing claims to seem superior, to avoid admitting that they are wrong, or to obtain some power. Shouldn't a literacy coach try to stop this behavior? I suggest that you don't. First of all, as a literacy coach, you might guess why individuals are making competing claims, but you don't know for certain. Second, if you try to overrule these individuals based on your assumption that they have questionable motives, you merely perpetuate the power struggle and the attempt to prove another person wrong. It would be wiser to respond to what the individuals have said, not what they may be thinking.

Address Intimidation. Literacy coaches occasionally find themselves working with dysfunctional groups in which one member intimidates others. This unhealthiness manifests itself in various ways. For example, group members may always agree publicly, even while disagreeing privately; the domineering group member may control the conversation by providing cues regarding what the others should say or believe; or disagreement on the part of any member may be treated with panic, rudeness, or by ostracizing him or her. Such situations happen temporarily in most groups, when addressing particular topics or when the group is just not at its best, but a truly unhealthy group has this problem consistently, and it is usually the result of one member.

This is among the most difficult group problems to address. Literacy coaches need to think carefully about these situations and might benefit from talking with trusted colleagues to get additional perspectives. Among the options available to literacy coaches are to ask the intimidating staff member to change his or her behavior or leave the group, or to encourage group members to change their manner of participating. However, each of these tactics is likely to backfire. A dysfunctional group does not correct itself easily. In fact, systems theorists tell us that all systems, including groups of people, have a primary function of preserving themselves; thus, the dysfunctional group is driven by self-preservation.

This is a discouraging picture. It frustrates me to have few successful tactics for literacy coaches in this situation. However, I do offer some advice. First, don't dismiss every group that struggles. The situation described in this section occurs only occasionally. Use all your best coaching skills with a group that is not going easily, and label it dysfunctional with caution. Get advice from a colleague who is also a coach before you give up.

Second, if there truly is an intimidator among participants, tune into that person in a calm, neutral manner. For instance, if someone uses abstract language and references to "the research" to quiet others from disagreeing, politely ask him or her to provide a minilesson to group members to bring them up to speed about the topic. Or if a group member conveys displeasure in what is occurring by sighing, looking at his or her watch, and jangling car keys (message: I can't wait to get out of here!), ask that person in a very quiet, neutral voice, "What's up?" These interactions are unlikely to produce visible results, but they acknowledge the intimidating party's behavior and invite the person to shift gears if something is truly amiss or if there really is something to share.

Third, in such instances, a literacy coach may suggest that the group split up, and the coach either coaches members as individuals or coaches some members as a small group and works with the intimidating person individually.

Finally, on occasion, a brave and patient literacy coach can ask the intimidating staff member for assistance, such as conducting a research review or providing an overview of what occurs in his or her classroom. This approach enables that staff member to feel valued and recognized. As you might guess, this approach can backfire by giving the intimidating staff member too much attention, but it might be worth a try.

The problem of an intimidating group member occurs only occasionally, but when it does, it can become the focal point of a group's functioning. Moreover, this problem can cause a literacy coach to feel overwhelmed and inept. I advise literacy coaches in these situations to dig deep into their coaching tool kits and make best use of every skill they have. In addition, I advise literacy coaches to stay calm and avoid taking anything that happens personally. Finally, I encourage literacy coaches to remember that the intimidating group member is still a human being, not a monster, and to approach that person in a humane and reasonable manner.

A Tool for PLT Development

I gained a great deal of insight into how PLTs develop over time when I read some research about the development of PLTs at two high schools in California. Professors Pam Grossman, Sam Wineburg, and Steve Woolworth (2001) received a grant to lead this project, and they were disappointed in how it went in the first year. However, as they studied over time the teams with which they were working, they came to understand that the teams were beginners in that first year and had characteristics that were different from more mature teams that had evolved over several years of working together. As a result, the researchers developed continua that charted the progress of teams over time. Here are three of their findings:

1. *Group identity:* PLT members start out identifying with only their friends in the group and sometimes don't value the others at all. Over time, pseudocommunity may develop, in which participants talk about being a community but don't really behave like one. Then, with time, the mature PLT becomes a place where everyone is valued and members identify with the entire group, even those from whom they are quite different.

2. *Understanding differences:* When the PLT is new, group members deny that there are differences, but over time their differences start to become evident, which makes members uncomfortable. As the group evolves, though, members recognize that conflict is inevitable and learn to deal with it honestly and even productively, as they come to value varying perspectives among members.

3. *Responsibility for members' growth:* Initially, PLT members seem concerned only about their own growth and maintain a focus on their students' learning rather than their colleagues'. With time, group members may start to value one another as resources, and when the group is mature, participants are likely to support one another's growth out of a sense of responsibility to one another.

These insights from the project of Grossman and her colleagues are helpful to coaches when they encounter a group that is functioning in a less-than-ideal way. The problem may be that the group just has not been together long enough and needs to evolve to a point where they are more effective together. Coaches might consider sharing this information with PLTs as a guide to how they might grow over time.

Conclusion

Partnering with PLTs demands many of the same skills as working with individuals. However, when working with groups, literacy coaches need to attend to interpersonal dynamics among group members and the tendency for group members to subconsciously want to maintain their roles and statuses and perpetuate the functional style of the group. In addition, the coaching cycle is altered a bit by the increased number of participants that are contributing to it.

The goal of small-group work, like the goal of individual work, is to assist participants in improving student learning by solving problems and pursuing topics of importance. In addition, PLTs increase collaboration among staff members. Such collaboration is occasionally marred by participants who are difficult to work with. This challenge has been touched on in this chapter but is addressed at length in Chapter 8.

ADDITIONAL RESOURCES

Achinstein, B. (2002). *Community, diversity, and conflict among schoolteachers: The ties that blind.* New York, NY: Teachers College Press.

Chandler, K., & the Mapleton Teacher-Research Group. (1999). *Spelling inquiry: How one elementary school caught the mnemonic plague.* York, ME: Stenhouse.

Greenleaf, C.L., & Schoenbach, R. (2004). Building capacity for the responsive teaching of reading in the academic disciplines: Strategic inquiry designs for middle and high school teachers' professional development. In D.S. Strickland & M.L. Kamil (Eds.), *Improving reading achievement through professional development* (pp. 97–127). Norwood, MA: Christopher-Gordon.

Wenger, E. (1998). *Communities of practice: Learning, meaning, and identity.* New York, NY: Cambridge University Press.

How Do I Address Specific Coaching Challenges?

CHAPTER 8

How Do I Deal With Difficult Situations?

- What should I do when a teacher refuses my assistance?
- How can I respond to rude behavior?
- How do I handle my worries about people who seem difficult?
- What should I do if I don't like the direction that the coaching partnership takes?
- Are there times when I should choose a teacher's goals?

Literacy coaching, like all work with people, provides interpersonal challenges. Literacy coaches themselves, because they are human, sometimes feel anxious or unsure. And the coaching conversation, because it presumes teachers' sincerity, insight, and commitment, sometimes disappoints. This chapter addresses common coaching challenges such as these.

What If a Teacher Is Resistant to My Support?

A major concern of literacy coaches is the resistant teacher, which is no surprise. If literacy coaches are in the business of helping teachers change, the most difficult part of the job naturally is those people who won't let the coaches do their jobs. Resistant teachers simply don't want to participate in the literacy coaching process.

What Is Resistance?

Let's reconsider what resistance means before suggesting ways for literacy coaches to work with it. Resistance is typically thought of as a negative behavior. Those teachers who resist are "poor" teachers. But let's reconsider that notion. Think about when you've resisted an initiative, whether at work, at home, in your community, or anyplace else. Why did you resist? I bet it was because you believed you were right on moral or intellectual grounds. You just knew that the idea was ill formed, you knew of research that demonstrated its weakness, or you were sure it was amoral or harmful. When we ourselves resist, we believe it is because we are good people who care about our work, communities, homes, and institutions. But when others resist, we often believe they are lazy, unconcerned, uninformed, or difficult. In other words, resistance is good in the eyes of the resister but bad in the eyes of those being resisted.

With this concept in mind, let's agree to make no judgments about the character of those who resist. Resisters are not inherently bad, even when they are resisting us. In the field of psychoanalysis, where the term *resistance* is commonly used, there is an understanding that resistance is a tool for growth. By examining why a person resists, one can learn more about that person's fears and motivations, the influence of the person's past, and the effect of the relationship with the analyst. In the process, growth occurs. This approach to resistance may be useful to literacy coaches as well, although I am not suggesting that literacy coaches act as psychoanalysts.

Having established that teachers who resist literacy coaches are not necessarily bad or ill motivated and that their resistance actually might be a source of information and growth, how do literacy coaches work from this perspective? The first step always should be to listen and learn. Table 7 includes some common statements that may seem resistant and suggested responses that literacy coaches might make.

Should I "Waste" Time Working With Resisters?

There's an adage in professional development circles that one should not waste one's time with resisters. I used to agree but have changed my mind. Literacy coaches can learn so much from resisters. First, literacy coaches can learn more about why teachers disagree with the literacy coaching model. This will help coaches either better explain themselves or try new approaches to the role of literacy coach. Second, literacy coaches can learn what resisting teachers value, which usually reduces the distance between a resisting teacher and a literacy coach and between a resisting teacher and other teachers because they understand one another better and may find shared values among themselves. Third, by continuing to attempt a connection with teachers who appear resistant, coaches increase the chance that these teachers will once again develop hope in a collaborative professional partnership. In their book *The Art of Possibility: Transforming Professional and Personal Life* (2002), Rosamund Stone Zander and Ben Zander remind us that those who appear unengaged may actually be protecting themselves because they have been disappointed many times in the past.

Let me give an example from my own experience. I was working with a school staff that was debating the best approach to spelling instruction. The staff was divided between those who wanted to continue to use the traditional spelling program based on a spelling workbook and those who wanted to

Table 7. Statements That May Seem Resistant

A Teacher Says	You Say
"You're wasting my time."	• "I want this time to be valuable for you. What might happen during this conversation for it to be valuable for you?"
"Just tell me what to do."	• "I would never presume to know what you should do. But I'd be glad to partner with you to think about the options that are available to you."
"Why don't you just give me the answers?"	• "I know that you're an experienced professional. If answers were easy, you would have thought of them already. I hope we can partner to ponder this situation and consider possible answers together."
"I don't need your help."	• "I hear you. Can you tell me a bit about your class and your successes?" • "A partnership might be about learning together or developing new ideas. It doesn't necessarily mean you couldn't do it without me."
"My students are all successful."	• "Great! Tell me about them."
"I've been teaching for 25 years, so I don't need a coach."	• "Tell me more." • "As a coach, I want to partner with you to focus on enhancing your students' success. We can all use a partner in this challenging work!" (And perhaps add: "Our partnership might focus on a particular student, an area of the curriculum that you're working on, or an interest you'd like to pursue.")
"Why don't you just come to my classroom and teach a group of students?"	• "Tell me more." • (And perhaps: "When you think about the learning that you want those students to do, and the teaching that you want to do, what gets in the way?") • (And if pushed: "My schedule doesn't allow me to come regularly to work with a group of students, but I'd be glad to problem solve with you about them.")

teach spelling based on words encountered in the content areas and in the students' own writing. After debating instructional methods and materials—both formally at a staff meeting and informally in after-school hallway conversations—the staff and I sat down to discuss their and my beliefs about spelling instruction.

This discussion led to our realization that we had many of the same beliefs. Where we disagreed was in how to implement those beliefs. We also learned the source of some individuals' strong support for one or the other approach. In one case, a teacher wept as she told the group of her own son's struggle to spell and of her belief that elimination of the spelling workbooks would lead other students to experience the same kind of struggle. The outcome of all of this sharing was that members of each side of the debate had greater understanding of the motivations held by those they were seeing as resisters, and we agreed to a statement of principle about what we all valued in spelling instruction.

When we listen to and learn from resisters, the conversation is richer, the differences often are blurred, and we usually can honor one another as people and teachers even if we still disagree.

I believe the notion of not wasting time on resisters was actually developed in response to the amount of attention a negative teacher can consume from someone such as a literacy coach. For instance, if a literacy coach selects one teacher who is very resistant as the measure of his or her success, the coach may spend an inordinate amount of time trying to change that teacher, which will lead to frustration and a lack of time for the other teachers. So, the idea of not wasting time might be rephrased as don't let a resisting teacher consume all of your time and energy. Do spend time listening to and learning from that teacher, but don't consider that teacher as the gauge of whether you've been successful.

When You Feel Uncomfortable

Literacy coaching is not easy work, and almost every coach feels defensive or anxious at some point. Practice being centered in the present moment so you can recognize these feelings when they arise, and can respond appropriately.

Anxiety

If you are feeling defensive, you are probably on the receiving end of a teacher's anxiety. Teachers have a lot to be anxious about these days, and sometimes coaches are merely convenient people on which to let loose. However, coaching itself can lead to greater teacher anxiety, particularly if a coaching program is represented as solving teachers' problems or "reforming" the school. Unskilled coaches make matters worse when they use poor communication skills or are unable to set their own needs aside in the coaching partnership.

Think about a time when you felt anxious, say, when interviewing for a job, giving a speech, or waiting in a doctor's office. Everyone experiences anxiety a little differently; some people perspire and get a stomachache, whereas others feel it in their back and shoulders. Some find it hard to focus, and others find themselves with tunnel vision, able to think only about the matter at hand. However you experience anxiety, you likely understand that no one enjoys the feeling and that everyone wants to get rid of it. In coaching situations, teachers' anxieties may lead to the "hot potato" effect, in which teacher partners get rid of their anxiety by tossing it to you, like a hot potato that they have picked up and want to pass on before it burns their hands. This phenomenon is evident when a teacher says something like, "This meeting is just a waste of time," and you find yourself becoming defensive as you "catch" the teacher's anxiety and try to justify the meeting and coaching in general.

When you find yourself uncomfortable in dealing with a teacher partner, consider that they may be anxious. I am not suggesting that you psychoanalyze the other person; rather, just remind yourself that your feelings may be the result of your partner's feelings and see if you can do anything to lessen anxiety. Here are some tactics that you might use:

- Tune in. As in most coaching situations, learning more about your partner's perspective is valuable and can help you find out what might be making him or her unsettled.

- Avoid defensiveness. When you yourself feel anxious, it may be difficult not to become defensive. Work to avoid taking personally whatever your teacher partners are saying or doing.

- Stay in the present moment. If you are present with your teacher partners, you will hear them better and be able to put the situation in perspective. If you stray into worrying about the past or future, you likely will have a harder time responding appropriately. For instance, if a teacher partner says he or she would rather not work with you anymore and you are present in the moment, you will recognize a need to tune in to learn about the teacher's concerns and perhaps develop a plan for taking a break in your collaboration without severing the relationship entirely. (Or, you may tune in and find out that the teacher is overwhelmed and needs a coach partner more than ever!) If, on the other hand, you get caught up in what could have been or might be, you may start to worry about what would happen if this teacher tells others about your conversation, or you may feel regret that you took on coaching duties in the first place. Such ruminations take you away from your coaching partner, lessen your ability to listen closely to what your partner is saying, and distract you from developing a good plan for how to move ahead.

- If possible, focus on aspects of the conversation that produce less anxiety. For instance, if you are working with a group of teachers who agreed to bring samples of student writing to the meeting and you hear them expressing nervousness about sharing those writing samples, you might pull back to a more general conversation about writing or look at some samples of writing from an online resource before team members turn their attention to the writing of their own students. This approach may help participants get comfortable with talking about student writing by using other tools before bringing their students' work into the conversation.

- Acknowledge anxiety. Have you noticed that when you become aware that you are anxious, your anxiety often lessens? Sometimes it helps just to say to a group something like, "I always feel a little nervous when I share my students' work for the first time." This can cause everyone to smile in recognition and become a little more relaxed.

Bad Behavior

Let's face it, there are times when even the gentlest person "loses it" and says something that is harsh, disruptive, or insensitive. Beyond lessening anxiety and avoiding their own defensiveness, savvy coaches will have in their tool kit some additional ways to respond, including the following:

- Slow down. You want to be careful about what you say and do, and giving yourself a few extra seconds and a few more deep breaths will help you act wisely.
- Give the benefit of the doubt. Zander and Zander (2002) suggest giving others, including people who are behaving badly, an A, meaning that one takes the perspective that colleagues are the kind of people who deserve an A for their work and their approach to it. Then, when things go wrong, one assumes that something is getting in the way of that colleague's success. In other words, get in the habit of assuming the best in your teacher partners so that when they struggle, you look for what is causing that struggle rather than what is wrong with them.
- Try a compassion practice. Follow the advice of some Buddhist teachers (e.g., Glaser, 2007) and tell yourself, "Just like me, this person wants to [be happy, be a successful teacher, do well, etc.]" Repeat it every time you think about the person causing you discomfort until you actually believe it.
- Get help. When you are unable to solve a relationship problem on your own, turn to a colleague. The best choice is usually another coach, whether in your school or district or even in a neighboring district. Another good choice, for those in large school districts, is the coordinator of the coaching program. Try to avoid other teachers in your school, and avoid the teacher's supervisor unless you feel truly threatened by the other person's behavior or language.

Concerns About Goals: What If a Teacher Has Poor Goals?

When I suggest to coaches that they begin with where teachers are and help teachers address their own goals, coaches are sometimes skeptical. They often worry about what they will do if a teacher develops a poor goal or no goal. This section addresses these concerns.

Distinguishing Poor Goals From Different Goals. Sometimes teacher partners develop goals that literacy coaches disagree with. To coaches, these goals usually seem poorly contrived, perhaps because the goals seem unlikely to solve the problem at hand or likely to lead to greater problems. At other times, coaches are troubled by goals that contradict their own beliefs about students, learning, and teaching. Look as honestly as possible at your response to goals that seem poor, and ask yourself, Are the teacher's goals poor, or are they merely different from my own? This is a tough question. If you are passionate about teaching and literacy, you surely feel strongly about the beliefs you hold, and therefore, you know that you are right. I'm the same way. But as I continue to grow, I find that most often when I don't want to consider ideas that compete with mine, I am motivated by fear. I'm fearful that the ideas I've dismissed just might have merit, even just a little bit of merit, and this doesn't feel good.

We humans are sense-making beings. Our brains work hard to make sense of our world. If we think we've figured something out, especially something as important to us as teaching and learning, we want to hang on to it. We don't want to have our sense making disrupted by a competing view. In fact, there is a theory of brain organization that suggests that the oldest part of our brains (in evolutionary terms) encourages us to divide the world into two groups: those like us and those not like us (MacLean, 1990). The first group is the group we like and affiliate with; the other group is threatening to us, and we want to reject it. (You can see how this skill was essential for survival at one time. It was important for our ancestors to be able to distinguish those not like us, such as tigers, from those like us to avoid getting eaten. However, this same survival skill leads to problems today, when this fine-tuned skill often leads to prejudice as we distinguish those not like us—for example, those who have different beliefs about teaching or even about religion—from those like us.) From this perspective, considering the worth of a teacher's competing views is not only threatening to the sense we've made of teaching and learning but also threatening to our sense of how we fit into our world.

So, your first difficult task is to open your mind just a little bit further to allow that this teacher's goal may be different from yours but still worth considering. Your way of opening your mind may be different from mine, but my ability to consider others' perspectives from a less-rigid position has grown as my sense of self, my psychological centeredness, and my spirituality have grown. I encourage you to find your own ways to have a more open mind.

Of course, if you find that you and your teacher partners have differing but perfectly acceptable goals, you still face the challenge of working with a goal that you disagree with. Here are my suggestions for such situations:

- Don't try to pretend. You will not further a trusting relationship if you pretend that you agree with a goal when you really don't. If the teacher is at all familiar with your work and your values, he or she will know that you don't agree and are pretending to. Even if the teacher doesn't know your work, at some point he or she may find out that you don't agree, and the teacher will feel betrayed if you have pretended to agree up to that point. This doesn't mean that you should state your disagreement outright or even that you should say anything about your views. You might do so if you have a long-term and very trusting relationship with the teacher, but most often you won't. In the latter case, your language should be much more neutral. For instance, you might say, "It sounds as if you have several reasons for making that decision," rather than, "What a great idea!"

- Listen and learn. Find out why the teacher has set the goal. Use prompts and questions such as, "Tell me more about that," "What made you decide on this goal?" and "What will be different about your students if you succeed with this goal?" However, here's the challenge: You need to ask these questions with a truly inquiring mind. If you are asking with a judging mind, I can almost guarantee that your judgmental stance will be revealed in subtle changes in your voice.

- Establish your respect for the teacher's perspective and goal. Use language to make sure that the teacher knows you heard him or her. You might even restate the goal and the teacher's reasons for wanting to implement it. Roger Fisher and Daniel Shapiro (2006), leaders of the Harvard School for Negotiation, describe a human concern that people want to be appreciated, which means they know that they have been heard, understood, and valued. Fisher and Shapiro make clear that one does not need to agree with another person to convey appreciation.

- Recognize that most problems have more than one solution, and therefore the teacher's goal may have just as much merit—and success— as a goal you might develop in a similar situation. Approach the situation with curiosity and humility and remind yourself that, at worst, the goal will not lead to the intended outcomes, and then you can help your teacher partner develop a new goal.

An example may be useful. What follows is a scenario in which the literacy coach disagrees with teachers' goals but successfully partners with the team nonetheless.

Maria is a literacy coach working with a group of fifth-grade teachers in an elementary school setting. These teachers have always taught in self-contained classrooms but have set a goal of moving to a departmentalized approach in which each teacher will be responsible for one core subject: reading, science, social studies, or math. Writing will be taught across the curriculum. Maria thinks this is a poor idea because she believes in integrating the content areas with reading instruction as well as writing instruction, and she doesn't see that being possible with this departmentalized approach. She recognizes her negative response to the teachers' idea and decides to set it aside until she learns more.

"Tell me more about your decision to departmentalize," Maria says at her first meeting with the fifth-grade teachers.

"Well," begins Paul, "we've noticed that we shortchange the content areas of science and social studies. We think that by making me entirely responsible for social studies and Leslie entirely responsible for science, we'll be sure to teach all the subjects as necessary."

"Also," chimes in Dorothy, "Paul is the only male teacher at the fifth-grade level, and we think all the students will benefit from an opportunity to interact with him. At this age, the boys are really looking for male role models."

Maria responds, "I see. You want to departmentalize in order to give all subjects adequate time and also to enable all students to interact with Paul. Have you looked at any other options?"

"We have," explains Leslie. "We visited Turner Elementary, over in Edgewater School District, where they use an integrated curriculum approach. We loved it, but we don't think it will work here because we don't have enough time to plan together. Also, Turner has a great library and an excellent computer lab, so they have resources for inquiry projects that we don't."

"So," replies Maria, "you'd find an integrated curriculum exciting but don't think it will work here because of lack of time and materials."

"Yes," the four teachers respond.

"Well, as you know, I worked with an integrated curriculum when I taught over at Jefferson Elementary, and, like you, I thought it was great. But I understand that you don't think it's workable here. I support your decision to move ahead with departmentalization, but I'm wondering, would it be beneficial to look at aspects of the Turner Elementary program that you liked and see if we can think creatively about how to include them in a departmentalized program? That may or may not be possible, but I'd be happy to help you explore possibilities."

In this example, Maria listens and learns, and then she responds with support. Even though she doesn't agree with the teachers' decision, she recognizes that it is well thought out, and she decides to assist them in whatever way she can. She also uses a good coaching skill called "and, not or." In other words, she suggests that there may be a choice that enables the teachers to departmentalize and include some of the aspects of the integrated curriculum used at Turner Elementary. By doing so, she helps the teachers think of greater possibilities.

All literacy coaches can use strategies similar to Maria's. By listening, learning, asking careful questions, and keeping an open mind, literacy coaches can assist teachers even when their goals are different from the coaches'.

Identifying Poor Goals. There are indeed goals that teachers set that can only be described as poor. A few from my own experience come to mind. For example, I once visited a classroom where the students' desks were in an outward-facing circle on a permanent basis, which meant the students did not interact with or even see one another for hours at a time. I also knew a teacher who divided her classroom library into "boys' books" and "girls' books" and separated the books according to stereotypical norms so, for instance, girls did not have the opportunity to read books about sports or wild animals, although they were given books on household pets. And there are still far too many classrooms in which students are given punishments that involve writing the same sentence over and over again—often hundreds of times—and then the teachers wonder why the students aren't interested in writing.

If you are working with a teacher who selects a truly poor goal, I encourage you to take the following steps:

1. Listen and learn. As in the case of a teacher having a goal different from yours, when dealing with what appears to be a poor goal, begin by listening to the teacher and learning his or her reasons for choosing that goal. You may be surprised to find some heartfelt and well-thought-out reasoning. Often, you will find that you and the teacher share more in common than you might have guessed, but choose different ways to reach the goal. For instance, teachers who group students by ability and teachers who don't usually share a goal of helping all students achieve but disagree about how to meet that goal and what gets in the way of accomplishing it. When there is a common outcome, there is more room for discussion. Although you and the teacher may not share the same short-term goal, you may be able to discuss long-term goals that you do have in common and find some common ground for working toward them.

2. Be sure the teacher knows that you hear his or her reasons and honor his or her desired outcome. It is unlikely that you'll hear from the teacher that he or she wants the students to fail or be treated unfairly. Make sure that you and the teacher establish that you are both working for the success and well-being of the students.

3. Honestly, but gently, express your reservations. This is the tricky part. You might use one or more of the following strategies for this step:

- Cite an outside source. You might say something such as, "You know, this discussion makes me think of something I just read about a teacher who was trying the same thing. Can I look back at that and get back to you tomorrow about what she found?" If the teacher agrees, do just as you promised. Find the article or book and share the portion you mentioned with the teacher the next day. Be careful not to put pressure on the teacher to agree with what the piece says. You might want to merely give the selected portion to the teacher and ask to discuss it at your next meeting. In that way, the teacher will have time to read and consider it on his or her own before discussing it with you.

- Share your experience. You might say something such as, "I had the same concern when I taught third grade. I tried something very similar and was so surprised by what I found. There was an unexpected result." Explain the result and then leave some time for the teacher to reflect before responding. You might say, "I'm not trying to get you to agree with me, but could I ask that you think about whether the same thing might happen in your situation? Maybe we could talk about it some more next week?"

- State a reservation. This is where you need to use your most neutral tone of voice and your friendliest, and least condescending, expression. You might proceed by stating, "I value your goal, but I wonder if there might be some unintended consequences. I'm concerned that the students will get unequal opportunities to learn with this approach."

4. Ask what the goal will look like if implemented successfully. This tactic accomplishes two purposes: First, it gets the teacher to move beyond the plan to the effect of the plan. Sometimes at this point, the teacher realizes that it won't have the result that he or she intends. Second, if the teacher does go ahead with the goal, it gives you both a criterion by which to gauge the goal's effectiveness.

5. Ask the teacher to brainstorm other options, if possible. By this point, the teacher probably will have concluded that you are not fond of his or her goal, and you may be pushing too hard to ask the teacher to consider other options, but do so if you can. Otherwise, consider asking the teacher if you could look at the professional literature to see how other teachers have approached the desired outcome, to see if there are other options available.

Let's look at an example of how a literacy coach might successfully address a teacher who has a poor goal:

Donald is a literacy coach working with Ria, a first-grade teacher in a school in which the students come from low-income families who have recently moved to the United States. Most of the families came from Mexico, but a small group came from Russia. In virtually all cases, the students' parents speak English as a second language, but neither Donald nor Ria knows how capable the parents are in reading printed English. Ria recently attended a workshop in which the teachers in a suburban elementary school assigned all students the daily homework of reading with their parents for 15 minutes every evening. The school's test scores rose, and Ria returned to her school excited about implementing the same goal. In a conference, she shares the goal with Donald, who replies, "Wow, I hear your excitement about this reading homework program. Tell me more."

Ria responds, "The teachers at Oak Village School saw their test scores go up when they used it there. The kids read 3 times more books, and you know kids have to practice the skills and strategies they're learning."

"Boy, you're on target about the need to practice. I agree. How would you implement that goal here in your classroom?" Donald asks.

"I'd do the same thing," explains Ria. "My students would have a sheet that went home every Wednesday in the take-home folder, and they'd return it the following Tuesday. Parents would record the number of minutes they read with their children. Because these are first graders, the students could read to their parents or listen to their parents read."

Donald believes that Ria's plan is unethical because there is not an adequate supply of books for children whose parents do not speak English. He responds, "I wonder how the parents who don't read English would fare. Do we have enough books written in Spanish or Russian for them to be able to read to their kids?"

Ria responds, "I've thought about that. Most of these parents know English, and the children need to learn to read in English. If the parents can't read to the children, then those children will have to read to the parents. Maybe the parents can learn along with their children."

Donald replies thoughtfully, "I hear you that you want the children to read in English. I wonder what the research says about the best way to get them to practice at home. Would it be OK if I looked around a little bit and shared with you what I find? Maybe there are some modifications we could make to particularly address this unique problem."

"Well," says Ria warily, "I'd hate to mess around with a program that worked so well."

"Yes, we don't want to spoil a good thing," says Donald. "But perhaps there's a way we can add value. We have a unique group of students here, and it would be exciting if we can take a good program and make it excellent for our students' own needs."

"Sure," Ria says. "Let me know how I can make the program fit these students' needs."

OK, this conversation may seem too ideal to you. If the conversation doesn't quite sound like one you would have, please bear with me. I believe the ideas behind it—the use of good communication skills, seeking to add value ("and, not or"), and honoring a teacher's goals—all have merit, even if the script is a little stilted. All literacy coaches can use similar strategies when working with teachers who have poor goals.

In this section, I divided teachers' goals into "good but different" and "poor." By implication, there also are "good" teacher goals. All of these labels are judgments that are tricky and that you should make with caution. It is always best to listen and learn before labeling and to try to be open to changing your judgment over time. In addition, try to live with a less-than-ideal goal before you dismiss it. It is always easier to go back to a teacher and say, "You know, after thinking about our discussion and doing some reading, I wonder if we could revisit your goal," than to dismiss a goal outright and then try to start the conversation again.

Conclusion

It is essential for literacy coaches to have in their tool kits the skills for recognizing the reasons why teachers make literacy coaches unhappy, uncomfortable, or unsuccessful. In addition, literacy coaches need skills in relating to teachers with open minds, to learn about teachers' perspectives and respond appropriately. In this chapter, I attempted to identify the most difficult challenges in the work done by literacy coaches. Another set of challenges may arise, though, when coaches are asked to coach differently in support of school or district initiatives.

ADDITIONAL RESOURCES

DiPardo, A. (1997). Of war, doom, and laughter: Images of collaboration in the public-school workplace. *Teacher Education Quarterly, 24*(1), 89–104.

Evans, S., & Cohen, S.S. (2000). *Hot buttons: How to resolve conflict and cool everyone down.* New York, NY: Cliff Street.

Stone, D., Patton, B., & Heen, S. (1999). *Difficult conversations: How to discuss what matters most.* New York, NY: Viking.

CHAPTER 9

What Do I Do When the Coaching Program Focuses on Initiatives?

- What is my role as a literacy coach working in a school that is implementing Response to Intervention or the Common Core State Standards?
- Is the coaching conversation different when the focus is new initiatives rather than teachers' learning?
- What should I do when others, or I myself, disagree with a new initiative?
- Is it wise for me to serve as an RTI interventionist, providing instruction to struggling readers?

Coaching that is most transformative starts with teachers and supports them in their professional learning. Most of this book focuses on such coaching because my goal is to help coaches make the greatest difference. However, sometimes literacy coaches are asked to coach for initiatives. In these instances, coaches do not begin with teachers but, rather, with something new that is being implemented in the school, district, or profession overall. Right now, the initiatives getting a great deal of attention in the United States are the Common Core State Standards (CCSS) and Response to Intervention (RTI), and educators in other countries are facing similar initiatives focused on state, provincial, or national standards and on differentiating instruction for all.

This chapter provides information about how coaching for initiatives is different from the coaching described in the rest of this book. Zeroing in on the CCSS, the chapter helps coaches consider their stances in relation to Common Core implementation, provides coaches with strategies for supporting teachers' shifts, and offers suggestions for approaching disagreement with the standards. In relation to RTI, this chapter offers insight into the need to understand RTI well and encourages reconsideration of coaches' roles as interventionists.

Differences in Coaching for Initiatives

Coaching for initiatives is different in some ways from coaching as a partnership to support teacher learning. Significantly, the client is somewhat different. When coaches focus on support for teacher learning, their clients are their teacher partners. However, when coaches support initiatives, they have several clients, such as administrators, program coordinators, grant directors, and others responsible for something new in their school or district. If coaches are effective, they help a number of people succeed in bringing the initiative to life, even if the coaches are only working directly with teachers. Of course, teachers are still clients as well, but not the only clients.

Another difference is that the evidence used to indicate coaching success is different. When coaching is focused only on teacher learning, partnerships are successful when teachers meet their goals. However, when coaching starts with initiatives, success is marked by evidence that initiatives have been implemented as desired.

The coaching cycle is altered slightly as well. It still includes identifying a problem, understanding it, deciding to try something, trying it, and then repeating in a cycle of continuous improvement, but prior to identifying the problem, the initiative is considered. In other words, the starting point is not the teacher but the initiative, and from a consideration of the initiative, a problem is identified. The easiest way to shift the coaching conversation in this manner is to alter The Question. Instead of asking something like, "When you think about the reading and writing that you want your students to do and the teaching that you want to do, what gets in the way?" coaches ask, "When you think about implementing [the initiative] with success, and you think about your students' learning as a result, what gets in the way?"

Table 8 delineates the differences in these two purposes for coaching.

Despite the differences between coaching for teacher learning and coaching for initiatives, there are similarities as well. In both cases, teachers are the focus of the coaching conversation, and savvy coaches will support teachers in shifting their understanding as well as what they do. As illustrated by the alternative form of The Question above, the coaching cycle begins with a problem, although when the focus is an initiative, the problem grows out of that initiative. Of course, in both cases, coaches use their best skills and perspectives to create partnerships based on trust and facilitated by strong communication skills.

Table 8. Coaching for Different Purposes

	Coaching as Support for Teacher Learning	Coaching as Support for Initiatives
Client(s)	Teacher	Teacher, initiative, and leadership
Sign of success	The teacher meets the goal or solves the problem.	The program is implemented as planned.
Process	Problem, understand, decide, try	Initiative, problem, understand, decide, try

The remainder of this chapter focuses on the initiatives of the CCSS and RTI. If your school is not implementing either of these, you will likely benefit from the rest of the chapter nonetheless if any kind of initiative is being implemented where you work.

CCSS

By the time of this book's publication, most U.S. states will be well on their way to implementing the CCSS, and most literacy coaches will be expected to play a part in bringing the CCSS to life. To succeed in this role, coaches need to accomplish three tasks:

1. Frame their actions according to an appropriate stance.
2. Develop strategies for supporting the complex shifts that teachers are being asked to make.
3. Prepare for disagreements and differences in perspective.

This section helps coaches with all three tasks.

Stances

As the CCSS are implemented, coaches are being asked to take on a variety of duties, ranging from responsibility for much of the implementation of the CCSS to merely adding the Common Core to the possible topics that might be addressed in coaching conversations. I encourage coaches and those who support them to develop a clear stance toward their role in bringing the CCSS to life. Four possible stances are coach as instigator, coach as implementer, coach as facilitator, and coach as monitor. Each is addressed in the following sections.

Coach as Instigator. When literacy coaches adopt the stance that they are instigators, they accept responsibility for getting the ball rolling in their school. These coaches create awareness of the standards, establish the school's commitment to implementing the standards, create a vision for successful standards implementation, and guide the development of a plan for how that vision will be brought to life. A metaphor for this stance might be the Olympics torchbearer who runs up the stairs during the opening ceremonies and lights the torch to signal the start of the games; similarly, coaches in this capacity create excitement, represent the communal commitment to the endeavor, and signal the start of the initiative. These are important steps in implementing the CCSS, but they are much better left to the building principal. The stance of instigator assumes a level of authority that is more appropriate for administrators. For coaches, this stance will ultimately lead to difficulty because coaching is most successful when it is clearly separated from supervisory duties, and coaches are most successful when it is clear to teachers that coaches are "one of them." The instigator stance will lead others to perceive coaches as the people in charge of the standards, and being in charge is never what coaching is about.

Coach as Implementer. Coaches who assume the stance of implementer lead efforts to bring the CCSS to life in classrooms. A metaphor would be the guide for a tour of a foreign county, who makes all arrangements, creates a schedule, organizes participants for each day's events, and makes sure everyone gets there safely; similarly, coaches who are implementers develop units of instruction, select appropriate instructional materials, demonstrate lessons, and ensure that the CCSS are indeed addressed in every classroom. Many coaches take on this role with success, as evidenced by the presence of the CCSS in every classroom in their schools. Have you ever noticed, though, that when you travel with someone else who takes responsibility for every step along the way, you often are unable to find your way on your own when you return to that country? The tour guide sometimes eliminates the need for the traveler to truly get to know the country at any level of detail, and in a parallel fashion, coaching that bears responsibility for Common Core implementation often unintentionally lessens teachers' ability to implement the standards on their own.

Coach as Facilitator. When coaches assume the stance of facilitator, they recognize that it is the teachers' responsibility to implement the CCSS but that a coach can support this process by working alongside teachers as a partner. The metaphor of the partner who leads a dance is one I turn to often, as readers of this book already know. Coaches who are like dance partners are moving with teachers as they implement the CCSS, but never by taking a strong lead; rather, the coaches subtly provide direction, just as the lead in a ballroom dance subtly directs his partner with a bit of pressure on her shoulder or back, but always ensuring that they are moving together in elegant synchronicity. These coaches help teachers by using the problem-solving cycle to address obstacles to CCSS implementation.

Coach as Monitor. Coaches who take the stance of monitor usually do so at the urging of administrators who need their help. In this capacity, coaches note which teachers are appropriately implementing the standards and which are not and then share this information with those who are ultimately responsible for CCSS implementation, typically the school principal. A metaphor is the nurse who takes one's blood pressure before every visit with the doctor. Just as the nurse relieves the doctor of the time needed to perform this task and, sometimes, is better positioned to have a trusting relationship with the patient who needs counseling about such matters, coaches typically work more closely with teachers than administrators and therefore are well positioned to know how the CCSS are or aren't coming along in teachers' classrooms. It makes sense that coaches would be excellent sources of information and insight about progress toward CCSS implementation, and administrators are savvy to recognize this. On the other hand, as I have shared elsewhere in this book, coaches who influence principals' perceptions of teachers are inappropriately getting involved in supervisory matters and will find teachers' trust reduced as a consequence. So what's a coach to do? I encourage coaches to share *general* information about the implementation of the CCSS with administrators but to avoid specifics about any particular teacher or, in very small schools, any particular grade level or department. For instance, it would be appropriate for a coach to report that academic vocabulary is being addressed in at least 70% of the courses in the core departments of a high school but inappropriate to say that the two teachers who teach economics are not addressing academic vocabulary at all.

These four stances are summarized in Table 9.

Table 9. Coaches' Stances in Relation to the Common Core State Standards (CCSS)

Stance	Knowing	Doing	Being
Coach as instigator	How can I *get* teachers to develop understanding of the CCSS?	How can I *get* teachers to adopt strategies for implementing the CCSS?	How can I *get* teachers to shift their beliefs, values, and perspectives in relation to the CCSS?
Coach as implementer	How can I *guide* teachers in understanding the CCSS?	How can I *guide* teachers in implementing the CCSS?	How can I *guide* teachers in shifting their beliefs, values, and perspectives in relation to the CCSS?
Coach as facilitator	How can I *partner with* teachers to deepen their understanding of the CCSS?	How can I *partner with* teachers to develop strategies for implementing the CCSS?	How can I *partner with* teachers to shift their beliefs, values, and perspectives in relation to the CCSS?
Coach as monitor	Do *teachers understand* the CCSS?	Are *teachers implementing* the CCSS well?	Have *teachers made necessary shifts* in their beliefs, values, and perspectives?

Savvy coaches will reflect on the stance they wish to take in regard to the CCSS and discuss it with their supervisors. This conversation is important because confusion and conflict will result if coaches assume stances that are different from what their supervisors expect.

Shifts

The term *shift* is invoked by leaders of the CCSS movement to invoke the idea that these standards are not just the next in a line of standards, to be implemented without noticeable changes in teachers' perspectives or practices. Rather, the CCSS are intended to provoke major changes—that is, shifts—in what teachers do and how they think. The challenge for coaches comes in recognizing that the transformations implied by the term *shifts* are not caused by external forces. True, others can influence teachers in making significant shifts; however, the change really comes from within. It's like that old joke about how many psychologists it takes to change a lightbulb: one, but the lightbulb really, really has to want to change!

Wise literacy coaches avoid thinking about how they might *get* teachers to make shifts in relation to the CCSS. Rather, coaches will consider how to support those shifts as partners in the process of understanding and then implementing the Common Core.

The AIM model of teacher professional learning is helpful here. Recall from Chapter 2 that teachers' learning leads to changes in what they know, what they do, and who they are, as reflected in their beliefs, values, and perspectives. Savvy coaches consider how the CCSS shifts require learning that influences all three aspects and help teachers learn accordingly. An example may make this clear.

Many literacy coaches are helping teachers with academic vocabulary, a topic addressed in the CCSS. Coaches who have not considered the myriad kinds of learning that support a shift to teaching academic vocabulary are likely to move toward the obvious, visible change that such a shift requires: implementing instructional strategies for teaching vocabulary. Now, instructional strategies are truly helpful for any teacher who wants students to learn the vocabulary of an academic discipline. However, many times when teachers are taught instructional strategies alone, they fail to fully implement them in their classroom, or even when fully implemented, the strategies alone fail to do the trick. It may be that these teachers would benefit from additional learning: learning that changes their understanding and/or their beliefs, values, and perspectives and perhaps learning that changes additional behaviors as well.

For instance, in the area of behaviors, teachers who are most successful at helping students with academic vocabulary are not learning instructional strategies alone but also are learning how to select significant vocabulary from a text and how to find time to teach academic vocabulary. In the area of what they understand, these teachers are deepening their comprehension of how people learn new vocabulary and what vocabulary is important to learn. Related to the aspect of teachers' beliefs, values, and perspectives, teachers successfully addressing academic vocabulary may be learning to believe that academic vocabulary is important to all students' learning and that it is content discipline teachers' responsibility to help students learn such vocabulary.

These kinds of learning in support of a shift toward teaching academic vocabulary are illustrated in Table 10.

The point is that the shift asked by the CCSS in relation to academic vocabulary likely requires much more of teachers than merely learning instructional strategies, important as those strategies are. For literacy coaches, the work of coaching becomes a lot more difficult when the focus broadens from teaching teachers strategies to supporting teachers' learning about what they understand, do, and believe. However, this broadening of attention increases the effectiveness of coaches' work.

The coaching conversation remains an effective way to help teachers with all the learning required to make the CCSS shifts. Coaches might begin by asking this version of The Question: "When you think about implementing [the standard being addressed] in your classroom and consider the student learning that might occur, what gets in the way?"

In addition to the coaching conversation, teacher learning that alters *understanding* can be supported by sharing videos about the CCSS, discussing in small groups an article or online resource about the specifics of the CCSS, or inquiring with colleagues into one of the standards. Coaches can help by suggesting videos or reading materials or finding resources for inquiry. In addition, coaches can arrange formats for the ensuing discussions, such

Table 10. Learning Across All Aspects to Make a Shift

Key Shift	Learning Related to Teachers' Understanding	Learning Related to Teachers' Behavior	Learning Related to Teachers' Beliefs, Values, and Perspectives
Assist students in building academic vocabulary	• Develop insight into which vocabulary is most important for students • Learn how people learn new vocabulary	• Learn how to determine which vocabulary terms students need help with • Learn strategies for helping students learn new vocabulary • Find time to teach academic vocabulary	• Believe that teaching academic vocabulary is important to all students' learning • Develop the perspective that academic vocabulary learning is part of their own teaching work

as brown-bag lunches or after-school study groups, and can facilitate these discussions as needed.

Coaches can support teachers in altering their *practices* by arranging visits to other schools, providing demonstration lessons, facilitating lesson study groups, and arranging video-viewing sessions. Savvy coaches will prompt consideration of not only the behaviors required to implement new practices but also the thinking (e.g., When would I use this strategy? How will I know it is successful?) that is necessary for continued effective use of them and the beliefs, values, and perspectives that underpin the practices (e.g., What belief about reading is reflected in this practice? What does this practice assume about my students as writers? What makes me uncomfortable about implementing this practice in my classroom?).

In relation to altering *beliefs, values, and perspectives*, savvy coaches recognize that these aspects of teachers' identities evolve rather than change quickly and that there is little that can be done to address them directly. True, a coach can ask, "What do you believe about [a topic such as writing instruction or learning vocabulary]?" but such questions are usually answered vaguely or not at all. We educators are not accustomed to such conversations. Rather than addressing beliefs, values, and perspectives directly, coaches are wise to listen for moments when teachers share such matters obliquely in conversation and to honor such occurrences. For instance, a teacher of grade 3 students might comment that he or she finds most 8-year-olds to be too immature to write routinely over an extended time period, as recommended by the standards, and in response a coach might ask gentle probing questions such as, "Could you tell me what you have noticed?" or "What qualities do you believe a child needs to write in that way?" These questions, if asked sincerely and in a neutral tone of voice, provide an opportunity to explore the teacher's belief while still honoring it.

Another way for coaches to address the matter of beliefs, values, and perspectives is to demonstrate their own awareness of how such aspects of their teacher identities intersect with their consideration of the CCSS. For instance, in talking about how the CCSS emphasize the text as the source of meaning and deemphasize the transaction that readers have with the text and context in constructing meaning, I have shared with teachers that this perspective contradicts what I believe from my study of Louise Rosenblatt's work. As I share this, I am careful to do so in a reflective, problem-solving manner; despite my own struggles with this CCSS presentation of where meaning lies, I do not help teachers if I sound like I am dismissing the CCSS or suggesting that they dismiss them.

These strategies for helping teachers learn what is necessary for essential shifts are summarized in Table 11.

Table 11. Strategies That Literacy Coaches Might Use to Support Teacher Learning in Each of the Three Aspects of Identity

Learning Related to Teachers' Understanding	Learning Related to Teachers' Behavior	Learning Related to Teachers' Beliefs, Values, and Perspectives
▪ Have a coaching conversation ▪ View videos ▪ Read articles ▪ Examine online resources ▪ Study groups ▪ Inquiry groups	▪ Have a coaching conversation ▪ Visit other schools ▪ View videos ▪ Demonstrate in classrooms ▪ Engage in lesson study	▪ Have a coaching conversation ▪ Honor teachers' beliefs, values, and perspectives ▪ Ask gentle, inquiring questions ▪ Share one's own beliefs, values, and perspectives

Disagreements and Differences

The range of opinions about the CCSS is extensive and broad; some educators are pleased to find challenging standards that will guarantee a top-notch education for all students, whereas others perceive the CCSS to be regimenting and unrealistic. Coaches might work with school staffs that are split about the CCSS or find that some teachers are merely ignoring the new standards in the hopes that the CCSS will soon fade away. In addition, some coaches themselves feel concerned about the CCSS.

The information in Chapter 8 about difficult situations applies to these issues. In addition, though, there are a few things that literacy coaches may want to consider when working with the CCSS: rumors, passivity, and internal struggles.

Rumors. All large-scale education initiatives lead to rumors, and the CCSS are no exception. Teachers have become anxious as the CCSS are implemented in their schools, given that the Common Core documents challenge some long-held understandings about learning, teaching, and literacy, that some educators have found the CCSS are being imposed on them quickly in a top-down fashion, and that revelations of the politics behind the CCSS demonstrate involvement of anti–public education corporate elites. Conservative politicians have resisted the CCSS because the standards have been promoted by President Barack Obama and Secretary of Education Arne Duncan, whom conservatives resist at all costs. Additionally, parents have felt unsure about what the CCSS are or have been concerned about the new CCSS-related tests on the horizon. Each of these groups, then, is prone to creating or repeating rumors.

Savvy literacy coaches will become well versed not only in the CCSS themselves but also in the circumstances surrounding their development and implementation. The CCSS Initiative website includes a "Myths vs. Facts" page (www.corestandards.org/resources/myths-vs-facts); other websites, such as those of the National PTA, FairTest, and various state departments of education, provide additional information and clarifications about the Common Core. Coaches who familiarize themselves with multiple resources and bookmark them on their computers will be able to quickly check out the rumors that pass their way.

Passivity. Another challenge that is unique to the CCSS is some teachers' passivity toward them; these teachers usually have encountered multiple iterations of standards that they are to address and have learned to continue doing what they have always done while using the language of the newest standards to appear as if they are doing something new. In fairness, such a response may have been the best way to cope in those situations where teachers found themselves to be the recipients of numerous top-down initiatives. However, the demands of the CCSS require educators to engage significantly and to make the deep changes represented by the term *shifts*.

The challenge for coaches is that pushing hard for teachers to pay careful attention to the CCSS—whether as cheerleader or commander—positions coaches in the instigator stance discussed previously, and in the long run, this stance lessens coaches' effectiveness. What are the alternatives? I suggest three:

1. Coaches might discuss these matters with their principals, not to report on unengaged teachers by name but to consider an appropriate stance for the coach and to be clear about separating the principal's role from the coach's.

2. Coaches might begin their coaching conversations by asking, "When you think about starting to implement the CCSS, what gets in the way?" This question will imply that it is time to consider the CCSS.

3. Coaches might provide teachers with some of the materials on shifts required to implement the CCSS and invite the teachers to have brown-bag lunch discussions about the shifts. Even for those who don't participate, their awareness of the significance of the CCSS will be enhanced by their awareness of these lunchtime conversations and the responses that participants in the discussions will make.

Internal Struggles. As literacy coaches study the CCSS, they are likely to have some doubts about one or more portion, given that the standards are complex and address a range of instructional matters, that they reflect particular perspectives on literacy and literacy learning, and that their development was partly political. I suggest that coaches aim to be positive but real.

Being positive means recognizing that the CCSS have the potential to enhance teaching and learning if implemented well. It means acknowledging that the CCSS are here to stay and that it is time (in most schools in most U.S. states) to roll up our sleeves and make them work. And being positive means knowing that coaches are positioned well to help teachers make the most of this new initiative.

Being real means avoiding a false enthusiasm that makes others uncomfortable by its artificiality. It means continuing to use solid research and theory to inform practices, just as one has always done. And it means acknowledging that there are portions of the CCSS movement that one is unsure about or finds troubling.

The balance between being positive and being real sometimes feels like walking a tightrope. Wise literacy coaches will accomplish this balance with the use of a few good strategies:

- Use language precisely. You can still be a positive support for teachers' implementation of the CCSS even if you say something like, "I'm not sure I agree with the research cited to support the claim that frustration-level reading actually helps students read." You will have a hard time being a positive support if you say things like, "There is just no research base for those Common Core Standards!" The key is to avoid overstatements and to use qualifiers such as *some, sometimes*, and *perhaps* to limit the extent of the claim that you're making. If teachers think that you are dismissing all of the CCSS, they likely will not turn to you for help in bringing the standards to life; if teachers think you have studied the standards carefully and know the research well enough to know where there may be some questionable details, they likely will respect your assistance with the standards.

- Articulate both your positive approach and your realism about the CCSS. Let others hear your commitment to bringing the CCSS to life in classrooms and your perspective on how to do so practically. Avoid making this sound like you are in charge for the entire school or trying to tell others what to do; rather, express your perspective in light of your own work as a coach. For instance, one might say at the start of the school year, "I'm looking forward to supporting you [the teachers] in bringing the CCSS to life. The CCSS present both challenges and potential, and I know together we can sort out which is which."

- When you question something in the CCSS or related materials, do your homework to investigate further. Then, if you continue to feel troubled, talk it over with colleagues who are coaches or coach supervisors, to think carefully about your response before voicing it or acting on it in your school.

- If you are troubled by the CCSS to the extent that you cannot support their implementation, consider pursuing a different position. It will be nearly impossible in the next several years for coaches to succeed without supporting the CCSS. Therefore, you will be helping yourself as well as your colleagues if you take another position, whether as a coach in a private school that is not implementing the CCSS, in a role in your current school district that does not require attention to the CCSS, in a position outside of public pre-K–12 education, or if you are mobile, in one of the few states not implementing the CCSS.

- If your reservations about the CCSS are significant but you feel you can support their implementation nonetheless, take an active role in professional organizations to influence the ongoing conversation about the standards and to be positioned well when it comes time to revise them, which may occur several years down the road.

Just as the CCSS present challenges to teachers as they attempt to bring the standards to life in their classrooms, the CCSS also challenge coaches as they adjust their practices and perspectives in supporting the implementation of this major initiative. Coaches who are part of their own coach network or study group will be wise to reflect together on their roles, their strategies, and their responses to the challenges of the CCSS.

RTI

Just as coaches are involved in the implementation of the CCSS, so they are key participants in RTI programs. Savvy coaches attend to matters similar to those they attend to when working with the CCSS, such as the coach's role in implementation, strategies to support teaching learning, and skillful attention to disagreements. However, there are two additional tasks that effective literacy coaches will attend to when working with RTI: (1) a clear understanding of what RTI is and isn't and (2) optimal levels of involvement in intervention work. This section addresses both.

Understanding RTI

At this point, most school districts in the United States have been implementing RTI for several years and have provided numerous opportunities for educators to learn about the initiative. Therefore, readers may believe that it is unnecessary for me to urge coaches to understand RTI. I find, though, that many educators who *think* they understand RTI actually have many misconceptions or have forgotten key RTI concepts when they actually implement it. For coaches, a clear understanding of RTI will help them support teachers in realizing the potential of what Allington has called "our 'last, best hope'" for literacy education (Rebora, 2010, para. 6).

Many educators believe RTI is a system for identifying poor readers, putting them into small groups, and providing extra instruction to them during a special period of the day. Although this is one possible approach to RTI, it is far from the recommendations of many literacy leaders and ignores the vision of some states' RTI models. When coaches fail to understand what RTI could be in their schools, they help teachers perpetuate what amounts to little more than the old "ability grouping" approach to reading instruction, which has long been shown to be ineffective. On the other hand, when coaches support their schools in bringing RTI to life with a thorough understanding of what it is and how it could be implemented, they make this innovation one that optimally improves students' literate learning.

It is beyond the scope of this book to provide extensive information about RTI. I encourage literacy coaches to enhance their understanding of RTI by reviewing their own states' RTI model and the International Reading Association's (2010) free brochure *Response to Intervention: Guiding Principles for Educators.* This brochure, as well as links to state RTI websites and a number of other RTI sources, can be found online at www.reading.org/ Resources/ResourcesByTopic/ResponseToIntervention/Overview.aspx.

Coaches' Involvement in Intervention

Many literacy coaches provide instruction to students who are receiving Tier 2 or Tier 3 interventions. Given that these coaches often have master's degrees in literacy and a number of years' teaching experience, it is logical for them to provide such services. In addition, many literacy coaches, myself included, delight in being able to work with struggling readers, both because teaching children is our first love and because we know that we can almost always produce demonstrable results. However, I'm not convinced that coaches are working for optimal effectiveness when they provide RTI interventions.

First, there are practical issues when coaches are interventionists. Intervention work typically occurs on a daily basis, which means coaches must be in a particular place at a particular time every day for intervention. For most coaches, such a commitment leads to a trade-off: More time with students leads to less time with teachers, their primary clients.

Second, when coaches work with students, they use their expertise to limited effect. For instance, a coach who works with five students over the course of a semester has the net effect of improving the literacy learning of five students. A coach who works with 20 teachers over the course of a semester has a net effect of improving the literacy learning of all the students that those teachers teach presently and in the future; the net effect is the improvement of literacy learning for thousands of students.

Third, when coaches provide interventions for a few students in teachers' classrooms, they do nothing to increase the capacity of those teachers. On the other hand, when coaches partner with teachers to help them plan and implement interventions, the teachers' capacity is expanded as a result. This is coaching at its optimal.

Finally, there is evidence that RTI interventions are most effective when provided by teachers who know the students well (Tissiere & Lieber, 2012). Too often, the students who struggle most in school are forced to work with multiple teachers for core instruction, whereas students who find school easier stay in their own classrooms and work with their familiar teacher(s). This backward system can be turned around when coaches help classroom teachers provide interventions for those who need them most.

Coaches wishing to optimize their effectiveness will reflect on these matters with their colleagues and supervisors to determine how to make best use of their time. Sometimes coaches will recognize that their first choice of the most enjoyable job duty (i.e., working with students) is not the most practical in terms of effectiveness. While in the job of coach, their role is to help teachers enhance their capacities. I have written elsewhere (Toll, 2008) about difficult choices and about times when it may be best for coaches to make the perfectly acceptable decision to return to working full-time with students as a classroom teacher or reading teacher. While in the role as coach, though, serving as interventionist as well is often not the best decision.

Conclusion

Coaching for initiatives demands additional perspectives and practices for literacy coaches. Savvy coaches support the implementation of the CCSS and of RTI by knowing the programs well, choosing an appropriate role for themselves, and developing key strategies for building teachers' capacities to bring the initiatives to life. Coaches will have added success if they know themselves well and reflect on their own preferences and their own feelings about particular new initiatives.

ADDITIONAL RESOURCES

Allington, R.L. (2009). *What really matters in Response to Intervention: Research-based designs.* New York, NY: Pearson.

Calkins, L., Ehrenworth, M., & Lehman, C. (2012). *Pathways to the Common Core: Accelerating achievement.* Portsmouth, NH: Heinemann.

Fuchs, D., & Fuchs, L.S. (2006). Introduction to Response to Intervention: What, why, and how valid is it? *Reading Research Quarterly, 41*(1), 93–99. doi:10.1598/RRQ.41.1.4

Toll, C.A. (2008). *Surviving but not yet thriving: Essential questions and practical answers for experienced literacy coaches.* Newark, DE: International Reading Association.

CHAPTER 10

How Do I Survive This Job?

- How can I manage all the tasks of literacy coaching?
- How do I prevent myself from getting discouraged?
- Is there any hope for making a difference?

This chapter offers practices that literacy coaches can use to survive on the job. There is nothing unique about literacy coaching that would make the survival strategies different from those that you'd find for other stressful jobs. Nor is literacy coaching unique among people-related jobs in which being one's best directly influences the way one works with one's "clients."

Because most of the strategies in this chapter are familiar, I review each one rather briefly. This doesn't mean that they are unimportant: I suggest that ideas such as these are essential to literacy coaches, in fact. However, these ideas probably will serve more as reminders rather than new information for you.

Note Your Accomplishments

By the middle of the school year, many literacy coaches are wondering if their efforts are worth anything at all. They notice the teachers who have ignored their suggestions, they review student assessments that show great need, and they check their records and realize that there are a few teachers they haven't met with in months. Literacy coaches, like most people, are not satisfied until the job is finished. The difficult thing about literacy coaching, though, is that the job never is finished. If literacy coaches' work is to strengthen the ability of the staff to increasingly help students achieve literacy success, then literacy coaches will always have something else to do.

In a way, literacy coaching success is like writing improvement: If we look at a single piece produced by a struggling writer, we may find our attention going to the flaws in expression, the confusing details, the poor punctuation, or other negative attributes of the writing. But if we look at the student's work over time, comparing a current piece of writing with ones done six months, one year, and two years ago, we probably will be amazed at the writer's progress and excited by many aspects of his or her current effort. It's all a matter of perspective. I encourage literacy coaches to take a parallel approach to their work to develop a parallel kind of perspective.

So, literacy coaches, please take a few minutes every week to note the things you have accomplished. You might begin team and individual meetings with such observations, too, so everyone in the school can acknowledge the hard work that they do. In addition, note where you started and where you are now. Begin every semester with a review of your progress. In other words, pay attention to your accomplishments, not only what has yet to be done.

Find a Support System

Everyone needs a support system, which is at least in part why we have friends, spouses, or partners and why we stay in touch with family members and former classmates. I encourage literacy coaches to specifically nurture a support system of other literacy coaches or, if that's not possible, other educators in leadership positions. The key is that members of a literacy coach's professional support system should work outside of his or her school building. By developing support outside the school building, literacy coaches gain several advantages. First, coaches get a more objective perspective than they would get from people in the same school. Second, coaches increase the odds that what is said will remain confidential. Third, coaches avoid being seen as having "favorites" among the people with whom they work every day. Fourth, coaches benefit from widening their horizons and hearing what is happening in other schools and perhaps other districts.

Finding a support system of teacher leaders from outside one's building is usually easy if one teaches in a large school district. However, in a smaller school district, a literacy coach may have no counterparts. This is a good time to remember that the International Reading Association has active local councils throughout the United States, in Canada, and in many other countries. Also, the Internet can make literacy coaching collaboration possible across distances.

Focus on Feeling Centered

When I use the word *centered*, I'm referring to a sense that I get when I am focused on the moment at hand, grounded in what is going on right in front of me, and calmly poised to face whatever that is. Some people refer to it as "being in the zone." Many traditions of martial arts, athletics, or meditation place attention on the area of the solar plexus, just beneath one's belly button, as a location of solidness. Physiologically, this area is one's center of gravity when in a standing position. Psychologically, it can represent the core of one's sense of self. Spiritually, it can attune one to a source of energy, creativity, or being. Thus, you can think of being centered as important in a physiological, psychological, or spiritual dimension, depending on your personal beliefs.

I encourage you to focus on feeling centered as you engage in literacy coaching. You can do this by breathing in a way that allows your breath to go all the way down to the bottom of your lungs, causing the middle and lower parts of your torso to expand. Others prefer to engage in formal practices, such as yoga or qigong, to help them become more centered. Still others find that prayer of one kind or another will promote a calm feeling of being connected solidly with one's life and the spirit behind that life. (By suggesting these practices as a source of centering, I don't intend to downplay other purposes that one might have for doing them.)

Find Ways to Relieve Stress

Methods for relieving stress are available to almost everyone these days. Articles in newspapers and magazines, reports on television, and pamphlets at doctors' offices all provide suggestions, including getting enough rest and exercise, talking about what's bothering you, having a support system, developing close relationships, making healthy food choices, and keeping a positive attitude. We know what to do to relieve stress, so how come so few of us do it? I can't answer that question, but I can encourage you to take the above suggestions seriously and try to incorporate stress relief into your daily life.

Don't Own All the Problems

Literacy coaches work in environments in which many factors are out of their control. Students come to school hungry, teachers work too many hours, parents lose their jobs, the school district goes into debt, cartoon violence shows its influence on the playground, and so much more. Sometimes it's easy for literacy coaches to get so caught up in their work that they forget that failures are not always *their* failures.

Literacy coaches do important work, but that work is a small part of the education picture. When change is not occurring as literacy coaches wish, they should not give up. They should evaluate how they can do their work more effectively, but they should not take all the responsibility. My advice is to not feel responsible but to never stop trying.

Have Hope

My favorite survival tip for literacy coaches is to have hope. Literacy coaches try so hard and feel so much commitment, and they do sometimes wonder what it's all worth. My advice is to remember this: No matter how much you may disagree with other educators about teaching practices, classroom management, assessment, or anything else, what you have in common with them is that you all care about students. I really believe this. My career has given me the chance to work with thousands of teachers, and I have met only one who didn't care about children. (I'm pleased to tell you that she is no longer in the education field.) This is the source of my hope. As long as there are millions of adults going to work every day at least in part because they care about children, we can hope for anything. And this is where literacy coaches can be so important. When a literacy coach encourages a teacher by mirroring what teachers are doing—describing what he or she sees and hears a teacher doing successfully—and assuring that teacher that the teacher's work is of value, the odds increase that that teacher will continue to do work that demonstrates care for students and commitment to their success.

Conclusion

As literacy coaches struggle to do their jobs well, they would be wise to remember a few key survival strategies:

- Remember to breathe.
- Have hope.
- See the good.
- Take care of yourself.

Beyond these key survival strategies, literacy coaches would be wise to maintain perspective on their own goals and the parameters of their work. The Conclusion provides an overview of what coaches should and shouldn't do.

ADDITIONAL RESOURCES

Palmer, P.J. (2007). *The courage to teach: Exploring the inner landscape of a teacher's life* (10th anniversary ed.). San Francisco, CA: Jossey-Bass.

Sandholtz, K., Derr, B., Buckner, K., & Carlson, D. (2002). *Beyond juggling: Rebalancing your busy life*. San Francisco, CA: Berrett-Koehler.

What Do Literacy Coaches Do?
What Don't They Do?

- What do literacy coaches do?
- What don't literacy coaches do?
- What are some good questioning practices?
- How do I go about mirroring?
- How do I avoid taking on supervisory duties?
- Why is it harmful to judge teachers, and how can I avoid doing so?
- Should I observe teachers in their classrooms?

I debated with myself about whether this chapter should go at the beginning or the end of this book. I decided to place it at the end for two reasons: I want it to serve as a review of important duties for literacy coaches, and I want it to be an inspiration as readers proceed with their literacy coaching work.

As the title above indicates, I've divided literacy coaches' duties into what they do and what they don't do. Therefore, for ease, I've also divided the text according to those two categories: The first part of the Conclusion discusses what coaches do, and the latter part provides what coaches don't do.

What Literacy Coaches Do

Listen

If you've read all the previous chapters, you've noticed that I mention listening a great deal. When you're in doubt about what to do as a literacy coach, listen. In fact, listening is especially important when you don't know what to do because your hesitation is probably a sign that you need more information. In my personal and professional lives, I've never heard anyone criticized or disliked because he or she listened too carefully.

Ask Questions

If you doubt yourself as a literacy coach because you don't feel that you have enough expertise, then develop expertise in this one area: asking good questions. A good cue that you need to ask questions is when you have an uncomfortable feeling of being put on the spot by someone else. Clearly, at that moment, you don't feel ready to reply, so ask questions. If you are feeling put on the spot because you don't know how to reply to the person, asking more questions buys you some time and helps you narrow the issue, perhaps to something you can answer. If you are feeling put on the spot because you think you are being set up (as when a teacher asks, "What do you think about the textbook series we just adopted?"), asking more questions can help you understand the concern that is behind the issue raised. And if you are feeling put on the spot because the person's request was completely unexpected, inquiring further can allow you to understand the other person's thinking and perhaps even see how it connects to the topic at hand.

We all assume that we know how to ask questions, and I suppose we do to some degree. But the following types of questions seem more useful than others:

- Open-ended questions—those without a yes or no answer—usually are helpful because they encourage teachers to provide more information.

- Questions that leave room for a range of reflection are good in a group discussion. For instance, asking a study group, "What struck you as most useful for your teaching?" will produce more reflection than asking, "Do you think the book's suggestions on revision would work in your classroom?"

- Questions are best when they do not leave a person feeling defensive. For example, when a teacher says that he or she tried a practice and it didn't work, that person might feel attacked if you ask, "What's your proof?" However, the teacher may feel more comfortable if you ask, "What did you notice as you were trying it?" (See Chapter 5 for additional suggestions.)

Mirror the Teacher's Words or Actions

A literacy coach can play a valuable role by telling a teacher what the coach sees or hears. In other words, the literacy coach serves as a mirror for the teacher. Here's an example:

Deborah, a literacy coach, meets with Wes, a sixth-grade teacher. Wes bursts into the room. "I've had it!" he declares. "I've tried everything to get the kids to write. I've given them topics and let them pick. I've shown them dozens of examples of good writing. I've brought in an author and a journalist. I've let them do projects that they write about. I've let them write notes to one another. Nothing—nothing—works." Deborah responds as a mirror and says, "You're really frustrated. You've worked so hard to promote writing, and your students aren't interested."

In this example, mirroring takes the form of active listening. In other words, Deborah repeats what she heard Wes say, to make clear that she has heard him. Sometimes, however, mirroring provides a reflection of what a teacher is doing, not saying. For instance, when a teacher has totally revamped his or her readers' workshop time, it can be valuable for the literacy coach to serve as a mirror and note all the things the teacher has done. Such mirroring assures the teacher that his or her efforts are not going unnoticed and also reminds the teacher of just how much work he or she has done.

I find that mirroring is especially valued by teachers now, when so much of the public feedback they receive is negative. Teachers so often read in the newspaper and hear on television that they are not doing their jobs effectively and that others could do it better. It is important for those who support teachers, including literacy coaches, to mirror the teachers' efforts and their investment in their work.

Collect Data

Literacy coaches need to collect data at three levels. First, they need to be part of the team that looks at schoolwide data on literacy achievement. Certainly, this includes test scores, but it also includes data on use of the library, parent participation in literacy-related activities, professional development in literacy, and other evidence of a literacy-learning culture. Second, literacy coaches need to collect data on their own work. How do they know that they are making a difference? How do they know that their practices are effective? Data collection will assist in answering these important questions. Third, literacy coaches should sometimes assist teachers in collecting data. This is a tricky issue because some teachers may prefer that the literacy coaches be responsible for data collection related to those teachers' classrooms. However, this is inappropriate because collecting and using data are an essential part of effective teaching, and teachers need to know how to do it themselves. Rather, literacy coaches should assist teachers in planning for data collection and analyzing data, and literacy coaches may occasionally do the actual data collection when it is impossible for teachers to do so. For instance, if a teacher would like to gauge students' on-task behavior during readers' workshop, when he or she is busy with guided reading groups, the literacy coach may come to the classroom and collect data about student activity at five-minute intervals throughout the workshop time.

Provide Resources

When literacy coaches provide resources, such as books, teaching aids, professional articles, and computer software, they are not actually providing for substantial change. However, they may indeed be creating potential for deeper changes. In other words, by helping teachers have the resources they need—and by saving teachers the time needed to track down those resources—literacy coaches help teachers get ready to try new alternatives, which can be valuable in and of itself.

Providing resources appears to be one of the best public relations moves that literacy coaches can make. Perhaps because resources are visible, concrete, and often in short supply in schools, they remind teachers of the valuable service that literacy coaches can provide. Most literacy coaches have at least one story about a teacher with whom they were not successfully making a connection until the coach found some material resources for the teacher. That effort subsequently led to a deeper connection and more collaboration between teacher and coach.

Coaches perform a range of duties that support their key clients: teachers. Some of these duties, such as listening, questioning, and mirroring, require strong skills in relating to others. On the other hand, some of these duties, such as providing resources and collecting data, require content-related skills. Both sets of do's reflect the need for literacy coaches to be well versed in the process and content of their work and to continue to update and refine their skills as they proceed.

What Literacy Coaches Don't Do

Supervise

Literacy coaches who get pulled into supervisory duties will never have the trust of the teachers with whom they work. Teachers won't open up to a literacy coach if the coach's work in any way influences the teachers' performance reviews. However, despite the indisputable truth of this statement, literacy coaches often find themselves on the edge of supervisory roles. This occurs most often in one of two ways.

Sometimes, literacy coaches themselves are so upset with a teacher's behavior that they feel they must report the teacher to the supervisor. Literacy coaches often try to distance themselves from the supervisory act by making the report to a trusted supervisor and asking the supervisor to keep the coach out of the matter. Unfortunately, teachers frequently make the connection and see how their interactions with a literacy coach led to the supervisor's involvement. The following are a few strategies that you can use to tread these dangerous waters:

- Invite the supervisor to routinely discuss the work that teachers are doing with you, the literacy coach, when the supervisor has meetings with teachers. In this way, the supervisor knows what is going on without you needing to report it.

- Encourage the supervisor to ask teachers to select something related to the work that they're doing with you for the supervisor to observe when visiting their classrooms. Again, this takes you out of the loop but keeps the supervisor involved with the effort.

- If a team meeting is continually plagued by the negative influence of one member, invite the supervisor to attend the meetings and then provide feedback to the group about how it can function better. Such observations will give the supervisor information to subsequently reflect on in a supervisory meeting with the teacher who is providing the negative effect.

In all of these instances, your goal as the literacy coach is to involve the supervisor directly, instead of serving as a go-between for the supervisor and the teachers.

The other instances in which literacy coaches get pulled into the supervision process are those initiated by supervisors. Often, especially when they are unsure or afraid to act, supervisors will ask literacy coaches to perform supervisory duties with underperforming or difficult teachers. Because the best supervision models are formative—that is, they promote teachers' development rather than merely judge—the line between coaching and supervision is sometimes blurred. A literacy coach can spot the moment he or she crosses the line into supervision by noticing whether his or her interaction with a teacher has any direct bearing on the teacher's performance review. Note that I use the word *direct*. Of course, an effective literacy coach will help teachers improve their practices, and that will lead to stronger performance reviews, but this is not a direct effect. A direct effect would mean that a teacher must change as a result of coaching or else face consequences, or that a literacy coach must point out certain failings in a teacher because the supervisor does not want to tell the teacher directly.

A clearly written job description is an excellent tool for literacy coaches in these tough situations. So, too, is a strong supervisor for *every* coach, someone who will talk to the teachers' supervisor when conflicts of interest occur. Finally, some of these problems can be avoided by a frank talk between a literacy coach and the teachers' supervisor at the outset of their work together. If the teachers' supervisor understands the role of the literacy coach and the model of effective coaching, the supervisor will be less likely to bring the coach into a difficult supervisory matter.

Judge

It's difficult to get close to a teacher's work and not judge it. It's especially difficult given that most literacy coaches are experienced teachers with strong beliefs and values about the work of teaching. However, judging impedes a literacy coach's effectiveness. Clearly, a teacher who feels judged will be less likely to work with that literacy coach and will be vigilant and perhaps reticent when they do work together.

Halting one's judgments is a difficult task. I haven't accomplished it to the extent I'd like to, but I have gotten as far as I have by learning to be present in the moment at hand. If I'm working with a teacher and can be totally engaged with what is going on at that moment, I'm much less likely to slip into judging. I think this is because fear is often attached to judgment. I sometimes feel a need to judge a teacher as good or bad, judge a practice as successful or unsuccessful, or judge a classroom as pleasant or unpleasant because I fear that if I don't, I might let something slip by. In other words, if I haven't judged, then I won't be able to catch what's bad and fix it, and I myself will then be judged a bad coach. There's a cycle of fear being enacted. Of course, this entire notion of catching the bad and fixing it is contrary to the model of coaching presented in this book. That's one of the reasons I strive to be present and to avoid getting caught up in fear and my need to judge.

Another trap we so easily fall into is the belief that others cannot tell when we are judging them. Part of the reason we have this belief is that it is actually true about half the time. But for every person who is ignorant of our judgment, there is another person who has caught on to it, and people in the latter group are usually those who are closer to us. No matter what we say, our judgments reveal themselves in subtle ways, especially through body language and tone of voice. So, if you are a literacy coach who decides to hide your judgment rather than eliminate it, know that you'll be successful some of the time but not all the time.

Observe Teaching

It surprises many literacy coaches and teachers when I suggest that coaching should not be about the observation of teachers as they teach. Part of this surprise is due to the fact that a peer-coaching model that was popular in the 1980s and early 1990s emphasized just such observation of teaching. In that model, teachers paired up and used an approach to peer coaching that paralleled the supervisory model that was popular at that time; that is, they had a preobservation conference, the observation, and a postobservation conference. In other words, teachers behaved like supervisors to one another, except for the fact that they did not have control over one another's evaluations or conditions of employment. The centerpiece of this model was the observation of teaching by the person serving as the coach (although both members of the dyad performed each role reciprocally). This model leads teachers to assume that literacy coaches will observe them teaching, and in fact, many literacy coaches are puzzled about how they could possibly do their jobs if they didn't observe teachers teaching.

The problem with "coach as observer of teaching" is that it puts the literacy coach in the position of judge (see the previous discussion of judging in this chapter). In addition, it makes clear that there is a power differential between the teacher and the coach. The literacy coach, with his or her ability to observe and judge the teacher, is definitely more powerful. Finally, this approach demonstrates mistrust of the teacher, implying that the teacher's own reporting of what goes on in his or her classroom cannot be trusted.

Now, some teachers tell me that they actually request that a literacy coach observe them because they have a trusting relationship with the coach and really want feedback on what is happening in their classroom. If a teacher really wants the literacy coach to observe, I would never say that my opinion should supersede the teacher's desire. However, I'd also encourage the teacher and coach to think about whether this observation relationship is really necessary and whether it truly does not influence their work together.

My beliefs about this matter are informed by the thinking of Joyce and Showers. These researchers have done some of the most influential work on coaching in education. Many of their studies were done in the 1980s and 1990s, but their work continues to be influential today. In one study, Showers and Joyce (1996) concluded that if the observation of teaching is occurring in a coach–teacher relationship, the coach should always be the one teaching and the teacher the one observing. They saw benefit to this demonstration teaching, but they did not see that the benefit of the reverse—the coach observing the teacher—was worth the cost to the relationship between teacher and coach.

Serve as the Expert

Although this topic was discussed in previous chapters, let me remind readers that literacy coaches who behave as experts undo the coaching model. You can't coach someone if they think you have all the answers; you will end up tutoring them instead. Moreover, when you act as the expert, you convey the sense that there are easy and clearly identified answers to the difficult issues with which teachers struggle. This is inaccurate in some cases and disrespectful of teachers' own knowledge and efforts in all cases. Finally, the literacy coach who is an expert will sooner or later come upon a topic about which he or she is not an expert, and that will lead to an uncomfortable, although perhaps ultimately productive, need to divulge his or her lack of expertise.

Provide Pull-Out Services

Literacy coaches often are asked to work with individual students or groups of students on a regular basis. This work can be valuable to the school, especially if class sizes are large or there is a shortage of expertise in working with readers and writers. However, this is not coaching work. If you do such work, make sure your supervisor and others understand that it takes you away from coaching. This may be the best use of your time—perhaps you'll coach half the time and work with students the other half—so I'm not saying you shouldn't do it. My point is that no one should think that that work is coaching.

On the other hand, literacy coaches sometimes work in classrooms with small groups, often in a guided reading arrangement, in a manner that includes a combination of instructional services and coaching. Here's an example:

Larry is a literacy coach in an elementary school. The third- and fourth-grade teachers recently have begun implementing a readers' workshop approach and have asked him to spend one hour per day working with guided reading groups. There are two classrooms at each grade level, so Larry spends Mondays and Wednesdays in the third grade, providing 30 minutes of guided reading in each classroom, and does the same for the fourth-grade classes on Tuesdays and Thursdays. He recognizes that his role during much of this time is a provider of instruction, not a literacy coach. However, he also knows that this work furthers his literacy coaching duties in several ways. First, a classroom teacher occasionally sits in on his guided reading lesson, when the teacher is not working with a guided reading group him- or herself. Also, Larry has conferences with each classroom teacher on a regular basis about what the teachers are doing in their guided reading groups, the progress they observe the students making, and the makeup of the groups. These conversations enable Larry and the teachers to discuss ideas about ongoing assessment and to share ideas for strategy instruction. In addition, he is consistently the one who suggests moving students among guided reading groups to better meet their instructional needs; he is fairly certain that without his demonstration and reminders, the teachers would not move the students. In these ways, then, coaching enters into the work that Larry does while providing in-classroom instruction.

Literacy coaches often have a difficult time saying no to requests to work with students. This may be partly because the coaches love working with students and hate to turn down any requests. However, it also could be because the coaches are not adequately focused on their goals. If you, as a literacy coach, are asked to work with students, reflect on how such work would or wouldn't help you further your coaching goals, and then act accordingly.

It is no coincidence that the final section of this Conclusion addresses tasks that literacy coaches should not do. I repeatedly encounter literacy coaches who are doing just such tasks—supervising, judging, serving as the expert, observing teachers, or providing pull-out services—and don't know how to get out of them. My goal in ending with this information is to provide a final reminder to literacy coaches that they must be clear about what their jobs entail and then stick to those tasks whenever possible. Think of the tasks that literacy coaches don't do as bearing a road sign that reads, "Danger: Proceed With Caution." Many literacy coaches certainly survive even when they do such tasks, but the risk of resulting problems is great. If possible, it is best to avoid these tasks altogether.

Conclusion

The lists above are not definitive. Literacy coaches perform many duties that are not on either list. My purpose in mentioning the items in this Conclusion is to remind literacy coaches about the general thrust of their work. They are on the job to provide support, encouragement, and responsiveness to teachers. They are not there to do the principal's job or the teacher's job, and they are not there to make others impressed or uncomfortable.

Literacy coaching is exhilarating when it goes well. It's exciting to work alongside another professional to help students achieve. When literacy coaching doesn't go well, the temptation is to feel like a failure. Instead, I encourage you to enjoy the challenge and realize that coaching, like teaching, is about problem finding and problem solving. Literacy coaching is best when you approach it as your best self—someone who is kind, centered, open, and trustworthy. If you live your literacy coaching life with the belief that coaching is at heart about relationships and growth, not answers and authority, you will be a genuine literacy coach who is successful in supporting teachers. I hope you enjoy literacy coaching as much as I do.

ADDITIONAL RESOURCES

Every chapter in this book closes with suggested resources related to the ideas in that chapter. Here, I want to suggest a different kind of resource: yourself. Keep a log of your initiatives, thoughts, insights, questions, notes, and anything else that will serve as a record of your literacy coaching work. You might want to put the log in an accordion file with sections or create a digital file on your computer. Then, when you are seeking sources for assistance, you can include your log as a resource for information and solutions. Certainly, you want to benefit from others' work, but as your coach, I want to remind you of all that you know and to encourage you to trust yourself as well as others.

As your text-based coach, I'm interested in hearing what you think. Without a doubt, coaching is a reciprocal act, and I would like to learn from you about what you find helpful in this book and what you find unhelpful. My e-mail address is cathy@partneringtolearn.com. Please contact me with your comments.

A Narrative Bibliography: Where Do These Ideas Come From?

This is not a typical bibliography, as you already can see. It isn't a mere list of books and articles to which you can turn to read more. Rather, this Appendix provides information about the resources cited throughout the book. But even then, it's not your typical annotated bibliography. I hope instead to weave a brief narrative about significant ideas presented in each chapter. What I wish to do is extend our discussions from the previous chapters into this Appendix, chatting one more time about topics related to literacy coaching. My comments and the references I cite refer to specific sections or statements I make in a given chapter to which I direct your attention. Topics are organized by the order in which they appear in the chapters.

Introduction: What Is This Book About? Who Is It For?

Changes Over the Last Decade

Virtually every educator in the United States knows about No Child Left Behind, but readers who are very new to the field of education or from other countries can learn more at the U.S. Department of Education's website (www2.ed.gov/nclb/landing.jhtml). No Child Left Behind was the major federal influence on schools in the 2000s. It was responsible for a major increase in standardized testing of students and for the disaggregation of test results according to socioeconomic status, race/ethnicity, status as an English learner, and gender.

The U.S. government's enforcement of provisions under No Child Left Behind has been mitigated by Race to the Top, the federal education initiative of President Barack Obama's Administration. Race to the Top has been especially influential through its requirement that states' eligibility for major federal grants depends on their commitment to national standards and the use of measures of student growth as one of the tools for evaluating teachers and principals. These rules led to the adoption of the Common Core State Standards (CCSS) by most states and the development of two tests: PARCC, developed by the Partnership for Assessment of Readiness for College and Careers, and Smarter Balanced. At the time of this writing, the CCSS are being challenged by both conservative and progressive groups, but it appears that the standards will still be implemented across the United States. More

information on Race to the Top can be found at www2.ed.gov/programs/
racetothetop/index.html. Check the websites of individual state departments of
education to learn about states' rules for teacher and principal assessment that
includes student test scores.

Links to information on the CCSS and Response to Intervention (RTI) can
be found in the bibliography for Chapter 9.

Chapter 1: What Is Literacy Coaching?

The International Reading Association (2004) produced a position statement,
The Role and Qualifications of the Reading Coach in the United States,
which provides a useful resource for those trying to identify the duties of a
literacy coach and for those wishing to ensure that literacy coaches have the
needed knowledge, background, and experiences. This position statement
can be accessed at www.reading.org/General/AboutIRA/PositionStatements/
ReadingCoachPosition.aspx.

Literacy Coaching Supports Adult Learning

For more on characteristics of adult learners, visit LInC Online's Staff
Development: Adult Characteristics webpage at www-ed.fnal.gov/lincon/
staff_adult.shtml.

Related to the research on adult learners is the research on the construction
of meaning. Educators increasingly theorize that learning is a process of creating
understanding through an active constructive process and that this learning is
best done—or from some theorists' perspectives, only done—in social contexts
in which the environment contributes to that construction. To read more on these
ideas, look at the work of Fosnot (1996) on constructivism in general or a book
edited by Phillips (2000) for varied perspectives and critiques on constructivism.

Literacy Coaching Supports Partnerships and Collaboration

The Standards for Professional Learning of the organization Learning
Forward, which formerly was called the National Staff Development Council,
emphasize the value of collaboration for teacher learning. You can read all the
standards at learningforward.org/standards#.UkzHez-Jluk.

Professional Learning Rather Than Professional Development

The same Standards for Professional Learning referred to above also explain
the value of shifting one's term from *professional development* to *professional
learning.*

Literacy Coaching Leads to Reflection

Reflection is one of those tricky areas in which those who support teacher learning ask for reflection frequently, but reflection is not always what results. Ironically, the ability to reflect appears to be a natural human trait. A really practical book about supporting reflection in individual teachers as well as in collaborative groups is *Reflective Practice to Improve Schools: An Action Guide for Educators* (York-Barr, Sommers, Ghere, & Montie, 2006). I find helpful research on teacher reflection to be written by Zeichner and Liston (1996) and Schön (1987). These works give thorough overviews of what reflection in teaching looks like and how it can be fostered.

Literacy Coaching Supports Student Learning

In addition to the two large-scale studies mentioned in Chapter 1, there are many smaller studies of literacy coaching. Joyce and Showers have done the most to address the issue of coaching in general. Their work in the 1980s and 1990s demonstrated that coaching did indeed contribute to student achievement (Joyce & Showers, 1988; Joyce, Murphy, Showers, & Murphy, 1989). In the specific area of literacy, a study by the Foundation for California Early Literacy Learning (Foundation for California Early Literacy Learning, 2001) demonstrated that coaching had a positive effect on young students' literacy achievement. In addition, Killion (2003) reports that ongoing support for teachers was found to be essential in effective literacy programs, although that support varied from what might be called true literacy coaching to more superficial forms of support. Lyons and Pinnell (2001) report positive effects of coaching on literacy learning, and Norton (2001) provides a study showing that student writing improves dramatically as a result of a professional development model focused on coaching. In addition, Lapp, Fisher, Flood, and Frey (2003) describe a program in three high-poverty San Diego schools that included literacy coaching as 50% of reading specialists' duties, which led to a marked increase in student achievement.

Initiatives Supporting Literacy Coach Positions

In the 2000s, the Carnegie Corporation of New York supported literacy coaching as part of its initiative focused on adolescent literacy. The Alliance for Excellent Education funded the development of a white paper on literacy coaching (Sturtevant, 2003) and included literacy coaching in discussions about adolescent reading programs. Interestingly, these organizations are now focusing their attention on matters such as the CCSS and teacher performance assessments. I don't think this reflects a rejection of literacy coaching on their part but rather an indication that they have moved on to new topics getting national attention and supported by the political milieu. The value of good professional learning opportunities and of professional collaboration is still referenced in their reports on these other topics.

Reading First is no longer being funded by the U.S. Department of Education; however, to learn more about this initiative that greatly influenced literacy coaching in the early 2000s, go to www2.ed.gov/programs/readingfirst/index.html.

If you would like to learn more about the mentor-coaching initiative in U.S. Head Start programs, go to eclkc.ohs.acf.hhs.gov/hslc/hs/resources/pd/Organizational%20Development/Mentoring/MentorCoaching.htm.

Striving Readers was a federal program in the late 2000s to enhance literacy instruction in secondary schools, and it included funding for literacy coaches. Striving Readers is no longer being funded, but you can learn more about it at www2.ed.gov/programs/strivingreaders/index.html.

The LEARN Act has never been funded because it was never passed by Congress. However, included in the bill is the requirement that school districts receiving funding under LEARN would provide job-embedded professional development of the kind provided by coaches. You can read the content of this proposal at www.murray.senate.gov/education/LEARNact.pdf.

For more on literacy coaching as a support for teachers of English learners, visit the website of the National Association for Bilingual Education (www.nabe.org), which has links to articles and related publications about literacy coaching. The TESOL International Association website (www.tesol.org) provides information about professional development workshops that include literacy coaches and also links to the organization's publications, which occasionally include information for literacy coaches.

Chapter 2: How Does Coaching Lead to Change?

AIM Model of Professional Learning

I realized several years ago that we assume teacher learning as a consequence of literacy coaching, but we don't always make clear how it occurs and how it is influenced. This is an underresearched area of our work. I therefore undertook a deep study of professional learning, developed a prototype model, got feedback from leaders in the field (Parker Palmer, Etienne Wenger, Brent Davis, and Dorothy Holland), revised the model, and collected more feedback as I shared it widely with coaches, administrators, and teachers (see Figure 5).

Figure 5. The AIM Model

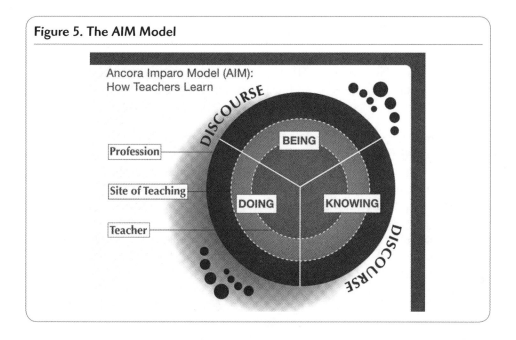

Ancora Imparo Model (AIM):
How Teachers Learn

DISCOURSE

Profession

Site of Teaching

Teacher

BEING

DOING

KNOWING

DISCOURSE

The following are key ideas represented by the AIM model (Toll, 2012):

- Teacher learning occurs in multiple "places" in our work—among individual teachers, yes, but also in classrooms, among school staffs, in the profession as a whole, and myriad other places.

- Teacher learning shifts what one knows, what one does, and/or who one is as an educator.

- Teacher learning is influenced by experience. For instance, a teacher's positive past experience in teaching English learners will influence the learning that teacher does when problem solving in a coaching partnership how to help an English learner currently in his or her classroom.

- Teacher learning is influenced by possibility. What a teacher believes is possible will shape what he or she learns. For instance, if a social studies teacher believes that all of her students can read and understand the Declaration of Independence, she will work with a coach to think about her lesson using this document differently than if she believes that only some students are capable of reading original source documents.

- Teacher learning is influenced by discourses that shape what it means to be a "good" teacher. Those discourses occur in popular media (e.g., movies about teachers), in legislation (e.g., No Child Left Behind), and in teachers' own professional communities. For instance, No Child

Left Behind introduced the rule that students would make Adequate Yearly Progress (AYP) based on test scores, so the discourse of teaching included the notion that "good" teachers ensured that their students made AYP. No matter whether teachers liked or hated this rule, it created a discourse that has shaped teacher professional learning. (See Gee, 2012, for more on the fascinating concept of discourses.)

Whenever a situation reflects two parts of this model that do not match up, there is disequilibrium and therefore the potential for learning. For instance, if a teacher's experience does not match the understanding in the profession as reflected in research, there is the potential for the teacher to learn, or on occasion, when many teachers' experience contradicts the research, a savvy researcher may recognize the opportunity for the profession (as represented by research) to learn. Another example would be an occasion when the beliefs of teachers at a school (e.g., about a particular group of students) contradict the beliefs of a new teacher there; perhaps all will learn.

Coaching partnerships can prompt healthy disequilibrium via the questions pursued, the multiple perspectives presented, and the opportunities to try something new. In these instances, teachers often find that their familiar understandings, practices, and perspectives are gently challenged by these good questions (asked by coaches or colleagues), alternate perspectives (presented by colleagues or when a team visits another site or team), or results of new initiatives. Thus, opportunities for learning occur.

Change Focused on Behavior. A book that provides an enthusiastic depiction of communication tools and attitudes for improving behaviors is *Whale Done! The Power of Positive Relationships* (Blanchard, Lacinak, Tompkins, & Ballard, 2002). Glasser's book, *The Quality School: Managing Students Without Coercion* (1992), applies his Choice Theory to education. The theory is based on the notions that genes drive our behavior and that our behavior focuses on moving from less pleasurable situations to more pleasurable ones. We choose our behavior, but our choices are dictated by this goal of experiencing more pleasure. When applied to coaching, Choice Theory would suggest that a coach should influence teachers' behaviors by making it pleasurable for the teachers to do what the coach wants.

A criticism of behavior-focused approaches to change, whether in schools, places of employment, homes, or society in general, is provided by Kohn (1999) in *Punished by Rewards: The Trouble With Gold Stars, Incentive Plans, A's, Praise, and Other Bribes.* He cites numerous studies that have demonstrated that behavior-focused approaches to change do not create lasting effects. An additional critique of change focused on behavior, in this case aimed directly at coaches, is in Flaherty's (1999) *Coaching: Evoking Excellence in Others.*

Change Focused on Attitude. A great deal of information about the Concerns-Based Adoption Model (Hord et al., 1987) can be found online at the website for SEDL, formerly the Southwest Educational Development Laboratory, at www.sedl.org/cbam.

I don't recommend coaching partnerships that focus directly on a person's beliefs and values, but should you decide to go in this direction, Whitworth, Kimsey-House, and Sandahl (1998) provide tools and protocols for doing so.

Change Focused on Cognition. The leading resource on coaching to change thinking is the work of Costa and his colleagues at the Thinking Collaborative who provide Cognitive Coaching Seminars. This work can be accessed through the Thinking Collaborative website (www.thinkingcollaborative.com) or the book *Cognitive Coaching: A Foundation for Renaissance Schools* by Costa and Garmston (2002).

National Writing Project

You can learn more about the model used to support teacher professional learning on the National Writing Project's (NWP) website (www.nwp.org/cs/public/print/resource_topic/professional_development). Essentially, the NWP is a network of educators who gather to write, reflect on their writing, and develop plans for how they can use those insights in their own classrooms.

Buddhist Concepts of Change

If you are interested in reading more about Buddhist concepts of change, you might want to read selections from *Nothing Special: Living Zen* (Beck, 1993), which provides transcripts of dharma (wisdom) teachings by a Zen teacher, or Mark Epstein's (1998) *Going to Pieces Without Falling Apart: A Buddhist Perspective on Wholeness*. The latter is especially written for someone who is not a serious Buddhist practitioner. Also, I have a chapter in *Spirituality, Action, and Pedagogy: Teaching From the Heart* (Denton & Ashton, 2004) that addresses additional insights on change that I have drawn from Buddhist teachings.

Significant Change in Education

The limited effects of many change efforts in education have been well documented by Tyack and Cuban (1995) as well as Gibboney (1994). These authors demonstrate that educational changes attempted throughout the 20th century had limited lasting effect, if any at all.

Problems With Demanding Change

Eaton and Johnson (2001) discuss the advantages of either a pull or push approach to coaching. The pull approach is one that is more demanding and places the coach in a supervisory role. Little (1990) analyzes teachers' responses to coaching and collaboration and notes that teachers frequently feel that asking for or needing help is a sign of inferiority. She stresses that collaboration, including coaching, is most effective when it occurs in a situation of interdependence among all participants.

Traumatic Change

Fournies (2000) includes in his book on coaching a discussion of the negative effects of traumatic change, which he refers to as punishment. He points out that this tactic for promoting change leads to the side effects of apprehension and aggression.

Respect

An intriguing analysis of many aspects of respect is Lawrence-Lightfoot's (1999) *Respect: An Exploration*.

Chapter 3: How Do I Influence Teachers?

Trusting Relationships

The importance of trust between coaches and their teacher partners is mentioned several times in this book. Bryk and Schneider (2002) have concluded that trust is essential for change in schools and have written about it in *Trust in Schools: A Core Resource for Improvement*.

Time for Coaching Tasks

Just about everyone in the modern world struggles to have enough time, and literacy coaches are no exception. There is no cure for this problem short of changing how we conceptualize time and work, which is not likely to happen soon. However, the book *Beyond Juggling: Rebalancing Your Busy Life* (Sandholtz, Derr, Buckner, & Carlson, 2002) provides a few tips that could apply to coaches, such as relying more on technology and delegating tasks that can be done by others.

It's Hardly Ever About Knowledge

The National Research Council (2000) produced a book, *How People Learn: Brain, Mind, Experience, and School*, that includes a chapter on teacher learning, including perspectives on the place of knowledge within other aspects of teachers' learning conditions.

Coaching and the Norms of the Teaching Profession

Coaches wishing to influence teachers might take a cue from a study done by Donaldson and her colleagues (2008), in which struggles of midcareer teachers were examined when they left the classroom to serve in a number of support roles, including coaching. The researchers found that many of the study participants' challenges resulted from the norms of the education profession, which prizes seniority, egalitarianism, and autonomy, but they also found that those who tried to *reform* teachers had large struggles. The takeaway for literacy coaches is to aim for influence, not reform!

Chapter 4: How Do I Begin My Work as a Literacy Coach?

First Impressions

The book *Reading People: How to Understand People and Predict Their Behavior—Anytime, Anyplace* by Dimitrius and Mazzarella (1999) includes a chapter on first impressions. It is written from the perspective of how first impressions can help one understand others, but in the process the authors demonstrate that first impressions do make a difference in how one is perceived.

Hubs

Davis and his colleagues (2007) give an overview of the kinds of networked systems that exist in any organization, including schools, and illustrate the effect of hubs.

Including Parents

Many resources provide suggestions for including parents in efforts to increase students' literacy achievement. These resources provide a range of perspectives on the role of parents and the relationships between parents and school personnel. Joyce Epstein and her colleagues (2009) have helped me consider that range of perspectives and understand the implications of various approaches to parents and parent involvement.

Chapter 5: How Can I Communicate Well?

Listening

Did you know that there is an International Listening Association? Visit their website (www.listen.org) for more information, including a list of 10 irritating listening habits. (Click on "Resources" and then "Education.") This list won't surprise you—it includes such annoying habits as rushing the speaker and trying to stop the speaker's story with your own—but it serves as a good reminder, which we all need occasionally.

Another excellent resource on listening is *The Lost Art of Listening: How Learning to Listen Can Improve Relationships* by Nichols (1995). If you're like me, you may think, I've known how to listen since I was born, so reading a book on listening would be like reading a book on breathing. First, remember that listening is different from hearing. Second, this book on listening is really a book on being the kind of person who makes connections with others. One of the author's insights that I found most helpful is that listening is really about suspending one's own needs. This is important for a literacy coach to remember because a literacy coach who is "listening" merely for an opportunity to interject his or her beliefs about what a teacher should be doing is not listening at all.

A third resource is Chapter 6 of *Reading People* by Dimitrius and Mazzarella (1999). This chapter provides a review of listening and questioning strategies. Two tips that I find particularly helpful are (1) to disclose a bit about yourself when another person is disclosing information about him- or herself and (2) to consider the context when another person tells you about a problem so you can recognize if the problem reflects the person's environment or if it is more chronic.

Questioning

Holcomb (2001) provides a series of questions and related protocols for stages in problem solving, which she divides into, Where are we now? Where do we want to go? How will we get there? How will we know we are getting there? and How will we sustain focus and momentum? These questions are close to the stages in the problem-solving cycle outlined in Chapter 6.

Communication Strategies

Tannen's work has influenced the thinking of many people regarding how humans communicate. She is probably most well known for her work on communication differences between men and women, but I have gotten a great deal of insight from her work on communication styles more generally. *Talking*

From 9 to 5: How Women's and Men's Conversational Styles Affect Who Gets Heard, Who Gets Credit, and What Gets Done at Work (Tannen, 1994) and *That's Not What I Meant! How Conversational Style Makes or Breaks Relationships* (Tannen, 1986) will be of particular interest to literacy coaches. Also, if you are working in a region where you did not grow up or are working with people from all over the United States or the world, you may want to check out Chapter 3 of *That's Not What I Meant!* because it details some differences in communication style that are geographically based.

Well–Chosen Words

A book by Benjamin (2008) offers phrases to use in myriad difficult situations, some of which might be encountered by literacy coaches. I'm sorry to report that not all of the solutions would fly in an educational milieu, even if they might in the corporate world. There are a few good tips, however, including acknowledge and plan, two steps to take when challenged by someone at a meeting: Acknowledge that you heard the person and then plan to talk about it outside the meeting. For instance, if a skeptical teacher challenges a coach at a staff meeting by saying, "This coaching business is just a waste of time!" it may be wise for the coach to reply, "I hear that you aren't convinced that coaching is worth your time. Could we talk about this after the meeting?"

Chapter 6: How Do I Facilitate Coaching Conversations?

Understanding the Problem

Mandinach and Jackson (2012) provide a history of using data for problem solving in education and offer protocols for making this happen. However, it is valuable to consider the work of the economist Dan Ariely (2009) before jumping on the data-driven decision-making bandwagon, because he is among those who have produced robust evidence that humans rarely make decisions based on data! It *is* important to use data in the coaching conversation, but it also is important to recognize that the sequence "data → decisions" doesn't always reflect reality. By inserting the *understanding* phase into the coaching cycle, coaches slow down the problem-solving cycle just enough to encourage collecting both a description of the problem and related data.

Goals

A good resource about goals related to student learning is Stronge and Grant's (2013) *Student Achievement Goal Setting: Using Data to Improve Teaching and Learning,* It provides processes and practices for setting goals, taking action to meet goals, and assessing whether goals were met.

Burke Reading Interview and Directed Reading–Thinking Activity

The sample coaching conversation recorded in the record-keeping sheets at the end of Chapter 6 includes references to the Burke Reading Interview (Goodman et al., 2005), which is a brief oral interview given to readers to learn what they believe reading is to be for and how they approach the reading process. The sample also refers to the Directed Reading–Thinking Activity (Rasinski & Padak, 2004), which is an instructional strategy that asks students to read silently and then predict what they will read next.

Additional Protocols

Coaches looking for protocols for coaching conversations beyond the one I have laid out in this chapter may want to look at *The Power of Protocols: An Educator's Guide to Better Practice* (McDonald, Mohr, Dichter, & McDonald, 2007).

Chapter 7: What Is Unique About Working With Teams?

When discussing professional learning teams (PLTs), literacy coaches sometimes have little theoretical understanding of how teams function or how they can enhance learning. Among all the resources that have helped me in this regard, Wenger's (1998) *Communities of Practice: Learning, Meaning, and Identity* has been the greatest help. Wenger has worked in pre-K–12 education, but his work extends beyond that. In this book, he discusses how people function in learning communities across a range of work settings, emphasizing that the defining characteristic of such communities is that they have a history of learning together. Wenger writes about the effect that work teams such as PLTs have on the participants' identities, the limitations of designing learning *for* teams, the tensions that exist between what practitioners experience in their work and what they are told about their work by "experts," the effect of possibility on learning, and other concepts that have influenced my AIM model of professional learning and my understanding of how PLTs function.

Learning Communities and Learning Organizations

To deepen your understanding of learning organizations, see Senge's (1990) book *The Fifth Discipline: The Art and Practice of the Learning*

Organization. To understand more about professional learning communities that encompass the entire school, read Dufour and Eaker's (1998) book *Professional Learning Communities at Work: Best Practices for Enhancing Student Achievement.*

Lack of Clarity

A number of authors have written about the pitfalls of collaborative efforts. Specific to the topic of coaching, Corrie (1995) found that when the "rules" of staff collaboration were unclear, the collaboration was unsuccessful and led to pseudocollaboration.

Tools for PLT Development

Here are some additional tools for PLTs that you may find helpful:

- Hargreaves (2008) reflected on the many PLTs he has worked with, and he identified seven kinds of teams, three well organized and committed to work that matters and four that are more about control or peer surveillance.

- Psychologist Wilfred Bion developed a theory that participants in groups at work focus either on the work at hand or on other matters, such as their hope for a better future situation or their personal needs. He found that leaders responded accordingly (see French & Simpson, 2010).

- *Difficult Conversations: How to Discuss What Matters Most* (Stone, Patton, & Heen, 1999) is an excellent book for sorting through the struggles that all groups have when they attempt to form teams. I know that some schools have used this book as a focus of staffwide discussion and reflection. This seems like an excellent idea to me because the suggestions in the book will be most effective when more than one person knows and uses them.

- The Anecdote blog site (www.anecdote.com.au/archives/communities-of-practice/) provides stories, tools, and insights about learning communities. One that I like is "Useful Conversations for Fledgling CoP" (Schenk, 2009), which offers activities that newish PLTs might use to enhance the work that they will do together by being clearer about who they are and why they are together.

- In her book *Community, Diversity, and Conflict Among Schoolteachers: The Ties That Blind*, Achinstein (2002) examines collaboration in two school settings and draws some useful insights. For instance, she suggests that collaboration leads as much to anxiety as productivity but that conflict may actually lead to healthier schools because it pushes staff members to think beyond their familiar comfort zones.

Working Across Differences

Ellsworth (1997) has one of the most thought-provoking perspectives on efforts to communicate and collaborate. Her background in film studies, combined with research from psychoanalysis, gives educators some unique perspectives on teaching and on what often is called communicative dialogue. She argues that such dialogue is never going to be completely successful, given the complexity of the communication act and the positioning of those participating. However, she urges educators to work difference, which involves recognizing that differences exist among collaborators, expecting and planning for conflict, acknowledging that there will be a struggle and that complete understanding will not take place, and doing the work anyway. Ellsworth suggests that rather than trying to eliminate conflict in collaboration, we should make it visible and include it as part of the work.

Chapter 8: How Do I Deal With Difficult Situations?

Resistance

My understanding of resistance has benefited from reading about it in works on psychology and on philosophy. The book *Working With Resistance* (Stark, 2002) informed me of psychologists' perceptions that resistance results from anxiety; an anxious person wants to avoid whatever seems to be reality to him or her, and this leads to resistance of psychotherapy or other forms of help. I have applied this notion to my work as a coach to recognize that people who seem resistant may be very anxious, and thus, I developed strategies to lessen anxiety-causing circumstances in coaching partnerships. The work of philosophers such as Judith Butler and Michel Foucault introduced me to the theories that embed resistance within power relations, meaning that resistance is a component of power, not opposition to power. For instance, in a coaching partnership that involves a PLT, one teacher may express frustration that the conversation turns to high-stakes testing, thereby shifting the conversation away from that topic and also increasing the power of that topic by making it somewhat taboo within the conversation of the team. Resistance can be both productive and counterproductive. This helps me as a coach to remember that what seems like resistance may be a way for a teacher to have some influence over a situation. I wrote about this in *Lenses on Literacy Coaching: Conceptualizations, Functions, and Outcomes* (Toll, 2007).

De Dreu and De Vries (1997) have done some fascinating work on the role of dissenters in organizations. They found that dissenters can help groups produce better work if they get group members to think differently about the topic at hand. However, De Dreu and De Vries also found that dissenters aren't automatically successful in creating such alternate or expanded views of the topic. The success of dissenters depends on a number of factors. Dissent will be most effective when dissent is encouraged in the group, when the dissenter is confident and respected by others on the team (because of their talent, because they have more power, or because they are part of an "in" group), and when the topic is of high importance to participants.

"And, Not Or"

Stone and his colleagues (1999), in their powerful book *Difficult Conversations*, suggest that participants in a difficult conversation break away from who's right and who's wrong and focus instead on the stories that each party has to tell. This is a useful step toward "and" rather than "or."

Anxiety and Bad Behavior

Assistance for working with people who are presenting themselves as difficult, anxious, or resistant is provided in droves by Scott (2004) in her book *Fierce Conversations: Achieving Success at Work and in Life, One Conversation at a Time*. She provides perspectives, questions, and strategies to help one remain focused and calm while moving beyond difficulties in partnerships. Another helpful resource is *Crucial Conversations: Tools for Talking When Stakes Are High* (Patterson, Grenny, McMillan, & Switzler, 2002), which, among other things, gives tips for responding when you are angry, keeping the conversation safe, and speaking persuasively.

Dysfunctional Groups

The book *Hot Buttons: How to Resolve Conflict and Cool Everyone Down* (Evans & Cohen, 2000) is like a master course on addressing conflict in groups. In fact, Cohen calls herself a "Conflict Coach." Using the techniques in this book may help you determine whether the group you are working with is hopelessly dysfunctional: If the techniques work at all, then the group may be able to function successfully, albeit with a little effort. Coaches dealing with dysfunctional groups also may find help in McClain and Romaine's (2002) *The Everything Managing People Book: Quick and Easy Ways to Build, Motivate, and Nurture a First-Rate Team*, which includes a chapter on addressing work group dynamics.

Chapter 9: What Do I Do When the Coaching Program Focuses on Initiatives?

Coaching for Initiatives

Le Fevre and Richardson (2002) conducted a study of teacher leaders who had coaching roles that involved leading the implementation of various early literacy programs. The researchers learned that these literacy coaches perceived a range of duties for which they were responsible. Some saw themselves as advocates for students or teachers, others saw themselves as visionaries, and still others saw themselves as monitors of quality assurance in the program implementation. These are just three of the considerable number of competing roles that Le Fevre and Richardson identified. Along with competing understandings of their roles, these teacher leaders differed in their understanding of what, if anything, they needed to change.

CCSS

Shifts. The concept of shifts in relation to the CCSS is laid out well on the EngageNY website (www.engageny.org). In addition, EngageNY provides tools that explain the shifts needed in both English language arts and math.

Resources for the CCSS. I routinely search for resources to assist coaches and teachers in understanding the CCSS and bringing them to life in schools, and I would estimate that the available resources double every six months. Therefore, I chose a few resources that are likely to remain available over time, but I encourage readers to do their own online searches as well. In addition, most state departments of education have created links to myriad CCSS resources.

- *Common Core State Standards Initiative (www.corestandards.org):* This website is sponsored by the National Governors Association and the Council of Chief State School Officers, the two organizations that led the creation of the CCSS. Note the "Resources" link at the top of the home page.
- *EngageNY (www.engageny.org):* In addition to the resources on teacher shifts described in the previous section, this website offers a range of additional tools, including tools for assessment progress in CCSS implementation, which coaches could share with teacher partners for their own self-assessment.
- *Illinois State Board of Education: The Common Core Professional Learning Series (www.isbe.net/common_core/pls/default.htm):* This

website offers professional learning materials at stages of implementation of the CCSS. Click on each level for a range of related tools and links.

- *NYC Department of Education: Tasks, Units & Student Work (http://schools.nyc.gov/Academics/CommonCoreLibrary/ TasksUnitsStudentWork/default):* This website of the New York City Schools provides units of study with performance assessments, all aligned to the CCSS.

- *Public Schools of North Carolina: NC Common Core Instructional Support Tools (www.ncpublicschools.org/acre/standards/common-core-tools):* This tool kit provides commentary on the English language arts standards by grade level. It consists of a chart listing each standard and gives suggestions for key components of instruction that bring the standard to life.

- *TextProject: Common Core State Standards Webinar Series (textproject.org/events/common-core-state-standards-webinar-series):* TextProject, funded by the State of California and led by Elfrieda Hiebert, offers a webinar series on the CCSS, with presentations by some of the leaders in literacy learning. One can participate when the webinar is presented live or view the archived videos and related materials.

- *Wisconsin Department of Public Instruction: Professional Learning on Demand (commoncore.dpi.wi.gov/learningondemand):* The Wisconsin Department of Public Instruction has created a series of professional learning modules related to the CCSS and using the LiveBinder platform for tools and resources.

- *National PTA (www.pta.org/advocacy/content2.cfm?ItemNumber= 3008&navItemNumber=557#):* The National PTA website provides suggestions for dispelling rumors about the CCSS as well as a link to participating states' resources for understanding the implementation of the CCSS in each state.

- *FairTest (www.fairtest.org/fairtest-infographic-common-core-more-tests-not-be):* FairTest provides a critique of the CCSS and the related assessments being developed by two consortia of U.S. states.

Rosenblatt's Work. Rosenblatt (1994) theorized that reading was the result of a transaction among the reader, the text, and the environment, contrary to the CCSS suggestion that reading results from the reader attending closely to the text.

Corporations and the CCSS. A flowchart that describes connections between the CCSS and corporations, some of them not necessarily supportive of public education, has been created in video form by Morna McDermott and posted on the website *Truthout* (see Bernd, 2013). It would be interesting to research each of the claims made by McDermott. Many of them are familiar to me, and I find them to be accurate; others are less familiar but intriguing.

Internal Struggles. Coaches who worry that they are compromising their beliefs, their mission as educators, or their relationships with their teacher colleagues might find help from a book called *The Compromise Trap: How to Thrive at Work Without Selling Your Soul* (Doty, 2009).

RTI

Understanding RTI. I find that many educators fail to understand the two common approaches to RTI, which Doug and Lynn Fuchs, leaders of the RTI movement, have labeled the problem-solving approach and the standard protocol approach. The problem-solving approach is one in which teachers collaborate with others, such as literacy coaches and special educators, to understand students and engage in a problem-solving protocol to determine the best instructional interventions for them. (This sounds like the approach to literacy coaching laid out in this book, doesn't it?) The other approach emphasizes fidelity to a program of intervention provided by a publisher. More on this and other aspects of RTI can be found in an article from *Reading Research Quarterly* (Fuchs & Fuchs, 2006).

The following are some additional resources that may help you understand RTI:

- *National Center on Response to Intervention (www.rti4success.org):* This website provides many resources and tools.

- *U.S. Department of Education: Smaller Learning Communities Program (www2.ed.gov/programs/slcp/2012thematicmtg.html):* The U.S. Department of Education sponsored a conference on RTI in 2012 and posted on this website the PowerPoints and handouts of all the presenters. This resource provides all the information that one could get from attending a conference—without the poorly prepared chicken luncheon!

- *"The Why Behind RTI":* In this article from *Educational Leadership*, Buffum, Mattos, and Weber (2010) offer perspectives on what really matters when planning for district- and building-based RTI programs. This resource is especially helpful to literacy coaches working with administrative teams or planning committees related to RTI.

- *"Responding to RTI":* Rebora's (2010) article presents an interview with Richard Allington, whose work on RTI and literacy is provocative and often spot-on.

- A Comprehensive System of Learning Supports Guidelines: This document from the Ohio Department of Education (2007) provides a great visual on page 7 that illustrates the range of supports that can be provided by RTI. It could be an excellent tool for helping to broaden the thinking of teachers and administrators who are stuck on the "sort the students by 'ability' and teach them differently for 30 minutes a day" approach to RTI.

- *California Department of Education: Resources-RtI²* *(www.cde.ca.gov/ci/cr/ri/rtiresources.asp):* The California Department of Education has identified 10 core components of RTI, such as high-quality classroom instruction, problem-solving systems support, positive behavioral supports, and professional development, and provides numerous resources for each.

Chapter 10: How Do I Survive This Job?

Stress Management

In his book *Connect: 12 Vital Ties That Open Your Heart, Lengthen Your Life, and Deepen Your Soul*, Hallowell (1999) provides a document that he originally prepared for the Department of Chemistry at Harvard University. In the document, he gives an overview of issues related to stress and how to address them.

I have also found assistance from Dave Allen, who has carved out a niche as the expert in helping people organize their work and their schedules. His complete plan for being productive, meeting all deadlines, and staying sane while doing so is laid out in *Getting Things Done: The Art of Stress-Free Productivity* (2001). Personally, I don't think the complete plan is something I want to take on, but I have benefited from several of the components of the plan. For instance, Allen suggests being specific when making a to-do list and itemizing only the very next step in a project. Thus, rather than writing on your to-do list, "Prepare for staff workshop on close reading," you might write, "Search the IRA publications catalogue for resources on close reading."

Feeling Centered

A large collection of audio files on mindfulness, from a variety of sources, can be found on the Free Mindfulness website at www.freemindfulness.org/download. You might also check out the many online resources from Jon Kabat-Zinn, an expert in stress reduction using mindfulness meditation. Likewise, there are many resources on yoga online. Eckhart Tolle's (2010) work also provides information on being centered. Tolle (no relation to me!) is not affiliated with any spiritual tradition, but he sees the connection between his perspectives and most spiritual traditions.

Conclusion: What Do Literacy Coaches Do? What Don't They Do?

Locating Resources

Among the many websites that can provide resources for literacy coaches are the following:

- *International Reading Association:* www.reading.org
- *National Council of Teachers of English:* www.ncte.org
- *Learning Forward (formerly the National Staff Development Council):* www.learningforward.org
- *Reading Rockets (funded by the U.S. Department of Education):* www.readingrockets.org, for resources on teaching young readers
- *¡Colorín Colorado! (funded by the U.S. Department of Education):* www.colorincolorado.org, for information on teaching English learners, particularly those whose first language is Spanish

Teacher Observation

If you absolutely must do observations of teachers in their classrooms because of a mandate that you can't get around, then you might want to read Lyons's (2002) chapter in *Learning From Teaching in Literacy Education: New Perspectives on Literacy Development*. She gives a step-by-step process for what she calls Analytic Coaching, a series of steps that a coach and teacher can use to guide the coach's observation and subsequent follow-up meeting with the teacher.

Peer Coaching

Showers and Joyce (1996) have written one of the best overviews of peer coaching. Their article is a bit old but was written at a time when peer coaching received a lot of attention.

Judging and Fear

Fear often leads to judging. I have thought a lot about the fear that we all feel at times as educators, and the detrimental effect it has on our work, since reading Palmer's (2007) book *The Courage to Teach: Exploring the Inner Landscape of a Teacher's Life*. I encourage you to place this book at the top of your reading list if you haven't read it already. Palmer's work continues to touch my heart and mind as I learn and grow in this profession.

This narrative bibliography provides sources of key ideas that have helped me develop my coaching practices. It also provides sources that you can turn to if you'd like to read further about some of the topics I've touched on. You may want to develop your own narrative bibliography in the form of a computer document or series of index cards to note important ideas that you get from your reading and the source in which you found them. Narrative bibliographies can be of great use for future reference. I hope this one serves that purpose for you.

REFERENCES

Achinstein, B. (2002). *Community, diversity, and conflict among schoolteachers: The ties that blind.* New York, NY: Teachers College Press.

Allen, D. (2001). *Getting things done: The art of stress-free productivity.* New York, NY: Penguin.

Ariely, D. (2009). *Predictably irrational: The hidden forces that shape our decisions* (Rev. ed.). New York, NY: HarperCollins.

Beck, C.J. (with Smith, S.). (1993). *Nothing special: Living Zen.* New York, NY: HarperCollins.

Benjamin, S.F. (2008). *Perfect phrases for dealing with difficult people: Hundreds of ready-to-use phrases for handling conflict, confrontations, and challenging personalities.* New York, NY: McGraw-Hill.

Bernd, C. (2013, September 6). Flow chart exposes Common Core's myriad corporate connections. *Truthout.* Retrieved from www.truth-out.org/news/item/18442-flow-chart-exposes-common-cores-myriad-corporate-connections

Biancarosa, G., Bryk, A.S., & Dexter, E.R. (2010). Assessing the value-added effects of literacy collaborative professional development on student learning. *The Elementary School Journal, 111*(1), 7–34. doi:10.1086/653468

Blanchard, K., Lacinak, T., Tompkins, C., & Ballard, J. (2002). *Whale done! The power of positive relationships.* New York, NY: Free.

Boorstein, S. (1995). *It's easier than you think: The Buddhist way to happiness.* San Francisco, CA: Harper.

Bryk, A.S., & Schneider, B. (2002). *Trust in schools: A core resource for improvement.* New York, NY: Russell Sage Foundation.

Buffum, A., Mattos, M., & Weber, C. (2010). The why behind RTI. *Educational Leadership, 68*(2), 10–16. Retrieved from www.ascd.org/publications/educational-leadership/oct10/vol68/num02/The-Why-Behind-RTI.aspx

Cave, J., LaMaster, C., & White, S. (2006). *Staff development: Adult characteristics.* Batavia, IL: Fermilab LInC. Retrieved from www-ed.fnal.gov/lincon/staff_adult.html

Chödrön, P. (2002). *Comfortable with uncertainty: 108 teachings on cultivating fearlessness and compassion* (E.H. Sell, Ed.). Boston, MA: Shambhala.

Corrie, L. (1995). The structure and culture of staff collaboration: Managing meaning and opening doors. *Educational Review, 47*(1), 89–99. doi:10.1080/0013191950470107

Costa, A.L., & Garmston, R.J. (2002). *Cognitive coaching: A foundation for Renaissance schools* (2nd ed.). Norwood, MA: Christopher-Gordon.

Cuban, L. (1998). How schools change reforms: Redefining reform success and failure. *Teachers College Record, 99*(3), 453–477.

Davis, B., Sumara, D., & Luce-Kapler, R. (2007). *Engaging minds: Changing teaching in complex times* (2nd ed.). New York, NY: Routledge.

De Dreu, C.K.W., & De Vries, N.K. (1997). Minority dissent in organizations. In C. De Dreu & E. Van De Vliert (Eds.), *Using conflict in organizations* (pp. 72–86). Thousand Oaks, CA: Sage.

Denton, D., & Ashton, W. (Eds.). (2004). *Spirituality, action, and pedagogy: Teaching from the heart.* New York, NY: Peter Lang.

Dimitrius, J.-E., & Mazzarella, M. (1999). *Reading people: How to understand people and predict their behavior—anytime, anyplace.* New York, NY: Ballantine.

Donaldson, M.L., Johnson, S.M., Kirkpatrick, C.L., Marinell, W.H., Steele, J.L., & Szczesiul, S.A. (2008). Angling for access, bartering for change: How second-stage teachers experience differentiated roles in schools. *Teachers College Record, 110*(5), 1088–1114.

Doty, E. (2009). *The compromise trap: How to thrive at work without selling your soul.* San Francisco, CA: Berrett-Koehler.

Dufour, R., & Eaker, R. (1998). *Professional learning communities at work™: Best practices for enhancing student achievement.* Bloomington, IN: Solution Tree; Alexandria, VA: Association for Supervision and Curriculum Development.

Eaton, J., & Johnson, R. (2001). *Coaching successfully.* London, UK: Dorling Kindersley.

Ellsworth, E. (1997). *Teaching positions: Difference, pedagogy, and the power of address.* New York: Teachers College Press.

Epstein, J.L., & Associates. (2009). *School, family, and community partnerships: Your handbook for action* (3rd ed.). Thousand Oaks, CA: Corwin.

Epstein, M. (1998). *Going to pieces without falling apart: A Buddhist perspective on wholeness.* New York, NY: Broadway.

Evans, S., & Cohen, S.S. (2000). *Hot buttons: How to resolve conflict and cool everyone down.* New York, NY: Cliff Street.

Fisher, R., & Shapiro, D. (2006). *Beyond reason: Using emotions as you negotiate.* New York, NY: Penguin.

Flaherty, J. (1999). *Coaching: Evoking excellence in others.* Boston, MA: Butterworth-Heinemann.

Fosnot, C.T. (1996). *Constructivism: Theory, perspectives, and practices.* New York, NY: Teachers College Press.

Foundation for California Early Literacy Learning. (2001). *California Early Literacy Learning, Extended Literacy Learning: Second chance at literacy learning* [Technical report]. Redlands, CA: Author. (ERIC Document Reproduction Service No. ED452510)

Fournies, F.F. (2000). *Coaching for improved work performance* (Rev. ed.). New York, NY: McGraw-Hill.

French, R.B., & Simpson, P. (2010). The 'work group': Redressing the balance in Bion's experiences in groups. *Human Relations, 63*(12), 1859–1878. doi:10.1177/0018726710365091

Fuchs, D., & Fuchs, L.S. (2006). Introduction to Response to Intervention: What, why, and how valid is it? *Reading Research Quarterly, 41*(1), 93–99. doi:10.1598/RRQ.41.1.4

Gee, J.P. (2012). *Social linguistics and literacies: Ideology in discourses* (4th ed.). New York, NY: Routledge.

Gibboney, R.A. (1994). *The stone trumpet: A story of practical school reform 1960–1990.* Albany: State University of New York Press.

Glaser, A. (2007, July). The hidden treasure of the heart. *Shambhala Sun.* Retrieved from www.shambhalasun.com/index.php?option=com_content&task=view&id=3106

Glasser, W. (1992). *The quality school: Managing students without coercion* (2nd ed.). New York, NY: HarperPerennial.

Goodman, Y.M., Watson, D.J., & Burke, C.L. (2005). *Reading miscue inventory: From evaluation to instruction* (2nd ed.). Katonah, NY: Richard C. Owen.

Grossman, P., Wineburg, S., & Woolworth, S. (2001). Toward a theory of teacher community. *Teachers College Record, 103*(6), 942–1012.

Hallowell, E.M. (1999). *Connect: 12 vital ties that open your heart, lengthen your life, and deepen your soul.* New York, NY: Pocket.

Hargreaves, A. (2008). Leading professional learning communities: Moral choices amid murky realities. In A.M. Blankstein, P.D. Houston, & R.W. Cole (Eds.), *Sustaining professional learning communities* (pp. 175–197). Thousand Oaks, CA: Corwin; Bloomington, IN: HOPE Foundation; Alexandria, VA: American Association of School Administration.

Holcomb, E.L. (2001). *Asking the right questions: Techniques for collaboration and school change* (2nd ed.). Thousand Oaks, CA: Corwin.

Hord, S.M., Rutherford, W.L., Huling-Austin, L., & Hall, G.E. (1987). *Taking charge of change.* Alexandria, VA: Association for Supervision and Curriculum Development.

Horton, M., & Freire, P. (1990). *We make the road by walking: Conversations on education and social change* (B. Bell, J. Gaventa, & J. Peters, Eds.). Philadelphia, PA: Temple University Press.

International Reading Association. (2004). *The role and qualifications of the reading coach in the United States.* Newark, DE: Author.

International Reading Association. (2010). *Response to Intervention: Guiding principles for educators.* Newark, DE: Author.

Joyce, B., & Showers, B. (1988). *Student achievement through staff development.* New York, NY: Longman.

Joyce, B., Murphy, C., Showers, B., & Murphy, J. (1989). School renewal as cultural change. *Educational Leadership, 47*(3), 70–77.

Killion, J. (2003). Use these 6 keys to open doors to literacy. *Journal of Staff Development, 24*(2), 10–16.

Kohn, A. (1999). *Punished by rewards: The trouble with gold stars, incentive plans, A's, praise, and other bribes.* Boston, MA: Houghton Mifflin.

Lapp, D., Fisher, D., Flood, J., & Frey, N. (2003). Dual role of the urban reading specialist. *Journal of Staff Development, 24*(2), 33–36.

Lawrence-Lightfoot, S. (1999). *Respect: An exploration.* Reading, MA: Perseus.

Le Fevre, D., & Richardson, V. (2002). Staff development in early reading intervention programs: The facilitator. *Teaching and Teacher Education, 18*(4), 483–500. doi:10.1016/S0742-051X(02)00011-2

Little, J.W. (1990). The persistence of privacy: Autonomy and initiative in teachers' professional relations. *Teachers College Record, 91*(4), 509–536.

Lyons, C.A. (2002). Becoming an effective literacy coach: What does it take? In E.M. Rodgers & G.S. Pinnell (Eds.), *Learning from teaching in literacy education: New perspectives on professional development* (pp. 93–118). Portsmouth, NH: Heinemann.

Lyons, C.A., & Pinnell, G.S. (2001). *Systems for change in literacy education: A guide to professional development.* Portsmouth, NH: Heinemann.

MacLean, P.D. (1990). *The triune brain in evolution: Role in paleocerebral functions.* New York, NY: Plenum.

Mandinach, E.B., & Jackson, S.S. (2012). *Transforming teaching and learning through data-driven decision making.* Thousand Oaks, CA: Corwin; Washington, DC: APA Division 15.

Marsh, J.A., McCombs, J.S., Lockwood, J.R., Martorell, F., Gershwin, D., Naftel, S., ... Crego, A. (2008). *Supporting literacy across the Sunshine State: A study of Florida middle school reading coaches.* Santa Monica, CA: RAND. doi:10.1037/e654542010-001

McClain, G., & Romaine, D.S. (2002). *The everything managing people book: Quick and easy ways to build, motivate, and nurture a first-rate team.* Avon, MA: Adams Media.

McDonald, J.P., Mohr, N., Dichter, A., & McDonald, E.C. (2007). *The power of protocols: An educator's guide to better practice* (2nd ed.). New York, NY: Teachers College Press.

National Institute of Child Health and Human Development. (2000). *Report of the National Reading Panel. Teaching children to read: An evidence-based assessment of the scientific research literature on reading and its implications for reading instruction* (NIH Publication No. 00-4769). Washington, DC: U.S. Government Printing Office.

National Research Council. (2000). *How People Learn: Brain, Mind, Experience, and School*. Washington, DC: National Academy Press.

Nichols, M.P. (1995). *The lost art of listening: How learning to listen can improve relationships*. New York, NY: Guilford.

Norton, J. (2001). A storybook breakthrough. *Journal of Staff Development, 22*(4), 22–25.

Ohio Department of Education. (2007). *A comprehensive system of learning supports guidelines*. Retrieved from education.ohio.gov/getattachment/Topics/Other-Resources/School-Safety/Building-Better-Learning-Environments/Create-Safe-Places-to-Learn/Guidelines.pdf.aspx

Palmer, P.J. (2004). *A hidden wholeness: The journey toward an undivided life*. San Francisco, CA: Jossey-Bass.

Palmer, P.J. (2007). *The courage to teach: Exploring the inner landscape of a teacher's life* (10th anniversary ed.). San Francisco, CA: Jossey-Bass.

Patterson, K., Grenny, J., McMillan, R., & Switzler, A. (2002). *Crucial conversations: Tools for talking when stakes are high*. New York, NY: McGraw-Hill.

Phillips, D.C. (Ed.). (2000). *Constructivism in education: Opinions and second opinions on controversial issues*. Chicago, IL: National Society for the Study of Education.

Pink, D.H. (2009). *Drive: The surprising truth about what motivates us*. New York, NY: Riverhead.

Rasinski, T., & Padak, N. (2004). *Effective reading strategies: Teaching children who find reading difficult* (3rd ed.). Upper Saddle River, NJ: Prentice Hall.

Rebora, A. (2010). Responding to RTI [Interview with Richard Allington]. *Education Week Teacher PD Sourcebook, 3*(2). Retrieved from www.edweek.org/tsb/articles/2010/04/12/02allington.h03.html

Rogers, C.R. (1989). *On becoming a person: A therapist's view of psychotherapy*. Boston, MA: Houghton Mifflin.

Rosenblatt, L.M. (1994). *The reader, the text, the poem: The transactional theory of the literary work*. Carbondale: Southern Illinois University Press.

Sandholtz, K., Derr, B., Buckner, K., & Carlson, D. (2002). *Beyond juggling: Rebalancing your busy life*. San Francisco, CA: Berrett-Koehler.

Schenk, M. (2009). Useful conversations for fledgling CoP [Web log post]. Retrieved from www.anecdote.com/category/communities-of-practice/

Schön, D.A. (1987). *Educating the reflective practitioner: Toward a new design for teaching and learning in the professions*. San Francisco, CA: Jossey-Bass.

Scott, S. (2004). *Fierce conversations: Achieving success at work and in life, one conversation at a time*. New York, NY: Berkley.

Senge, P.M. (1990). *The Fifth Discipline: The Art and Practice of the Learning Organization*. New York, NY: Currency.

Showers, B., & Joyce, B. (1996). The evolution of peer coaching. *Educational Leadership, 53*(6), 12–16.

Stark, M. (2002). *Working with resistance.* Northvale, NJ: Jason Aronson.

Stone, D., Patton, B., & Heen, S. (1999). *Difficult conversations: How to discuss what matters most.* New York, NY: Viking.

Stronge, J.H., & Grant, L.W. (2013). *Student achievement goal setting: Using data to improve teaching and learning,* New York, NY: Routledge.

Sturtevant, E.G. (2003). *The literacy coach: A key to improving teaching and learning in secondary schools.* Washington, DC: Alliance for Excellent Education.

Tannen, D. (1986). *That's not what I meant! How conversational style makes or breaks relationships.* New York, NY: Ballantine.

Tannen, D. (1994). *Talking from 9 to 5: How women's and men's conversational styles affect who gets heard, who gets credit, and what gets done at work.* New York, NY: William Morrow.

Tissiere, M, & Lieber, C.M. (2012, April). *Response to Intervention: What it is and how we do it?* Plenary session presented at the Strategic Interventions for Student Success Conference, Washington, DC.

Toll, C.A. (2005). *The literacy coach's survival guide: Essential questions and practical answers.* Newark, DE: International Reading Association.

Toll, C.A. (2006). *The literacy coach's desk reference: Processes and perspectives for effective coaching.* Urbana, IL: National Council of Teachers of English.

Toll, C.A. (2007). *Lenses on literacy coaching: Conceptualizations, functions, and outcomes.* Norwood, MA: Christopher-Gordon.

Toll, C.A. (2008). *Surviving but not yet thriving: Essential questions and practical answers for experienced literacy coaches.* Newark, DE: International Reading Association.

Toll, C.A. (2012). *Learnership: Invest in teachers, focus on learning, and put test scores in perspective.* Thousand Oaks, CA: Corwin.

Tolle, E. (2010). *The power of now: A guide to spiritual enlightenment.* Vancouver, BC, Canada: Namaste; Novato, CA: New World Library.

Tyack, D., & Cuban, L. (1995). *Tinkering toward utopia: A century of public school reform.* Cambridge, MA: Harvard University Press.

Wenger, E. (1998). *Communities of practice: Learning, meaning, and identity.* New York, NY: Cambridge University Press.

Whitworth, L., Kimsey-House, H., & Sandahl, P. (1998). *Co-active coaching: New skills for coaching people toward success in work and life.* Palo Alto, CA: Davies-Black.

Wolvin, A.D. (2010). Listening engagement: Intersecting theoretical perspectives. In A.D. Wolvin (Ed.), *Listening and human communication in the 21st century* (pp. 7–29). Malden, MA: Wiley-Blackwell. doi:10.1002/9781444314908.ch1

York-Barr, J., Sommers, W.A., Ghere, G.S., & Montie, J. (2006). *Reflective practice to improve schools: An action guide for educators* (2nd ed.). Thousand Oaks, CA: Corwin.

Zander, R.S., & Zander, B. (2002). *The art of possibility: Transforming professional and personal life.* New York, NY: Penguin.

Zeichner, K.M., & Liston, D.P. (1996). *Reflective teaching: An introduction.* Mahwah, NJ: Erlbaum.

INDEX

Page numbers followed by *f* or *t* indicate figures or tables, respectively.